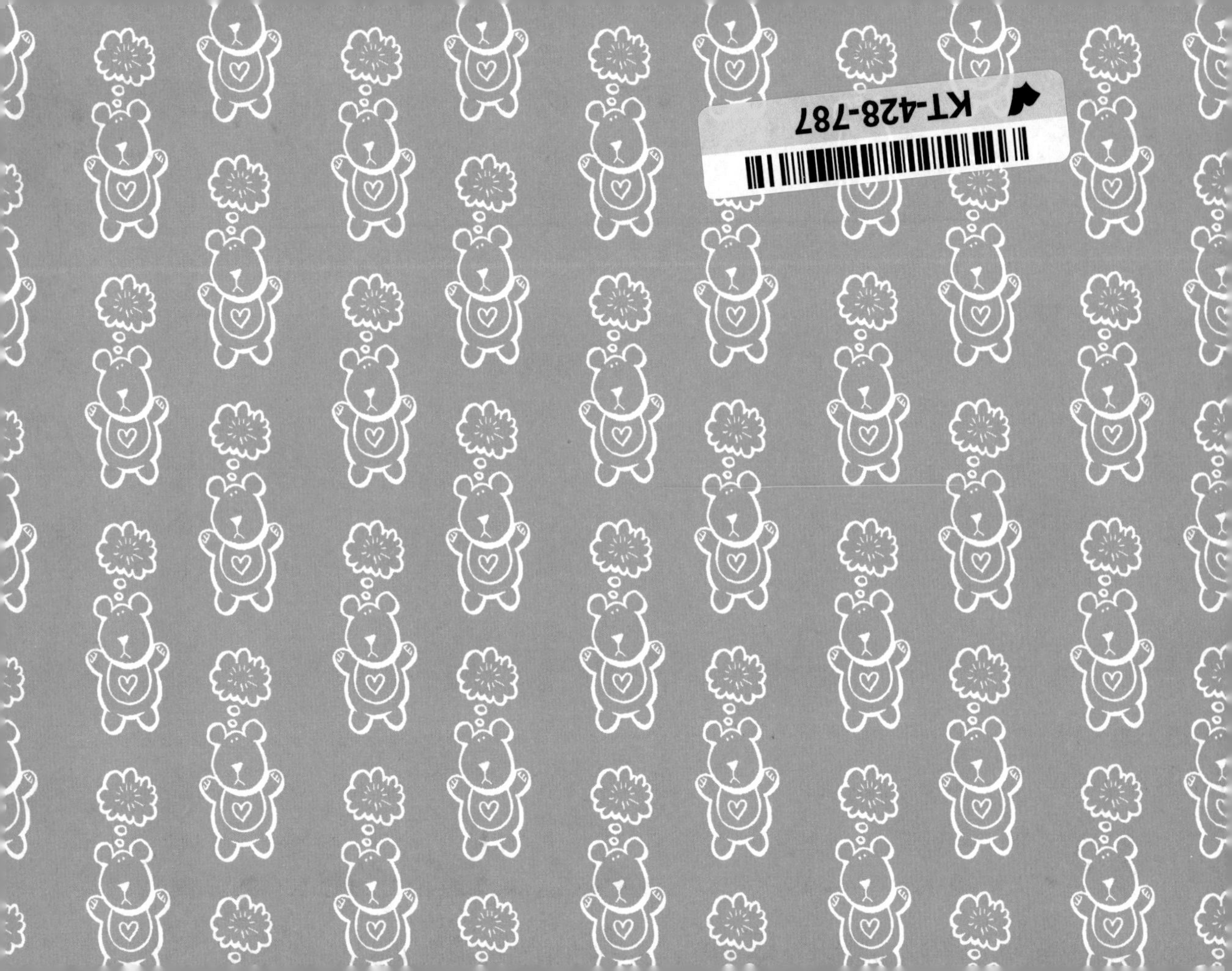

Loads More Lies to tell Small Kids

Andy Riley is the author of THE BOOK OF BUNNY SUICIDES and RETURN OF THE BUNNY SUICIDES and GREAT LIES TO TELL SMALL KIDS. He has written for Black Books, Little Britain, Smack The Pony, Trigger Happy TV, Big Train and The Armando Iannucci Shows. He is the co-creator of Hyperdrive, BBC2's new science fiction sitcom, and Radio 4's The 99p Challenge. His weekly cartoon strip, Roasted, runs in the Observer Magazine.

Loads More Lies to tell Small Kids

Andy Riley

HODDER &
STOUGHTON

Copyright © 2006 by Andy Riley

First published in Great Britain in 2006 by Hodder and Stoughton
A division of Hodder Headline

The right of Andy Riley to be identified as the Author of the Work has been asserted by him in accordance
with the Copyright, Designs and Patents Act 1988

A Hodder & Stoughton Book

1

A CIP catalogue record for this title is available from the British Library

Hardback ISBN 978 0 340 89964 6
Paperback ISBN 978 0 340 92365 2

Printed and bound by William Clowes Ltd, Beccles, Suffolk

Hodder Headline's policy is to use papers that are natural, renewable and recyclable products and made from
wood grown in sustainable forests. The logging and manufacturing processes are expected to conform to the
environmental regulations of the country of origin

Hodder and Stoughton Ltd
A division of Hodder Headline
338 Euston Road
London NW1 3BH

With thanks to:
Polly Faber, Camilla Hornby,
Kevin Cecil, Nick Davies
and all at Hodder & Stoughton

WHEN YOU CHANGE CHANNELS ON THE TV
THE PRESENTER YOU WERE JUST WATCHING
DIES INSTANTLY

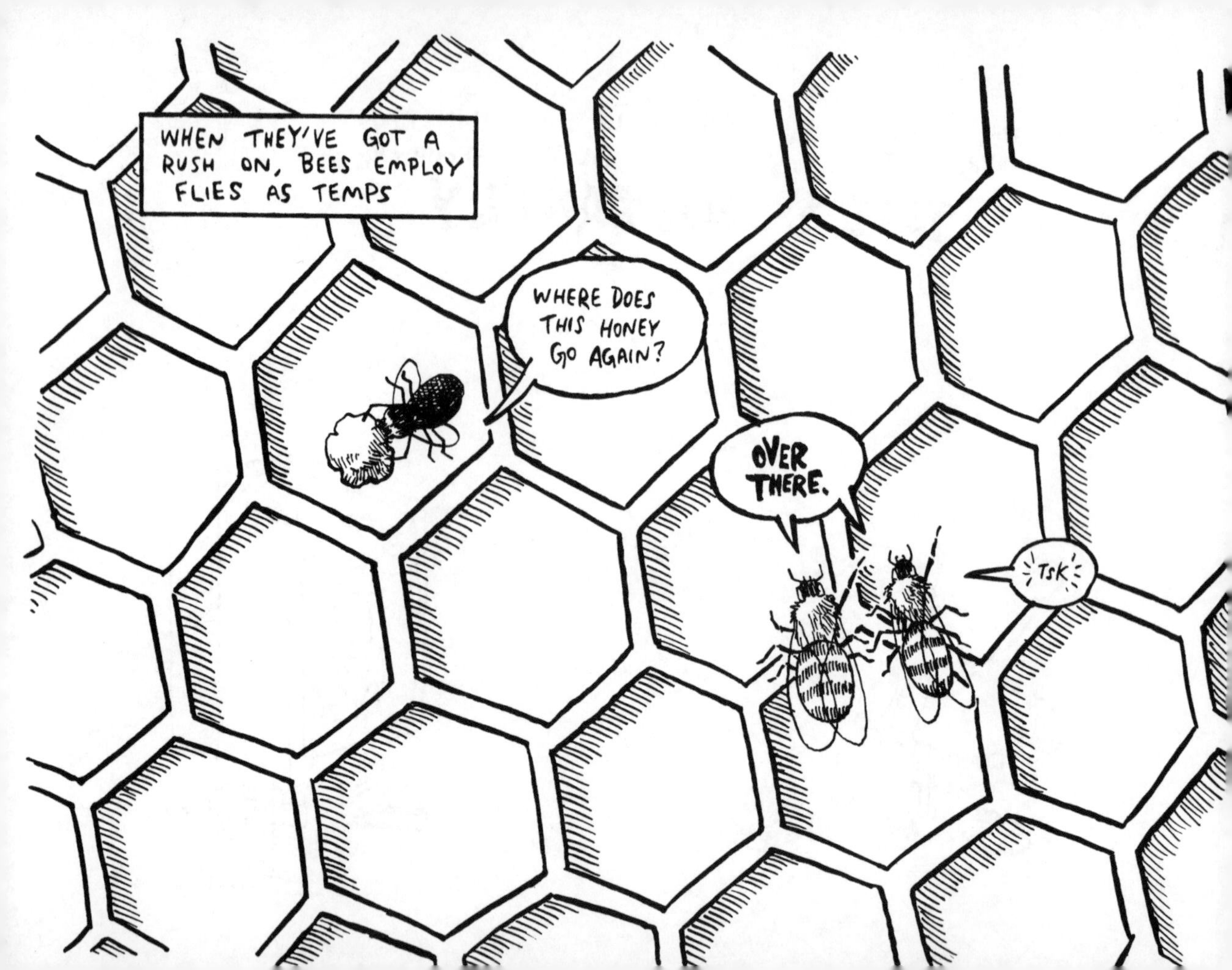
WHEN THEY'VE GOT A RUSH ON, BEES EMPLOY FLIES AS TEMPS
WHERE DOES THIS HONEY GO AGAIN?
OVER THERE.
TSK

IF YOU RUB TWO RED
HEADED KIDS TOGETHER
YOU CAN MAKE FIRE

ONCE EVERY YEAR

THE SPOTS ON
YOUR OLDER BROTHER'S
FACE SPELL OUT
HIS NAME AND
ADDRESS IN
BRAILLE

French people

EAT CROISSANTS

AND POO BAGUETTES

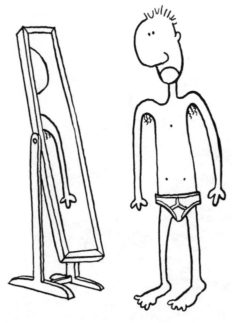

your dad's got one nipple and two belly buttons

THE ORIGINAL PURPOSE OF STONEHENGE WAS TO BE THE SETTING FOR THE VERY FIRST GAME OF "WHO WANTS TO BE A MILLIONAIRE"

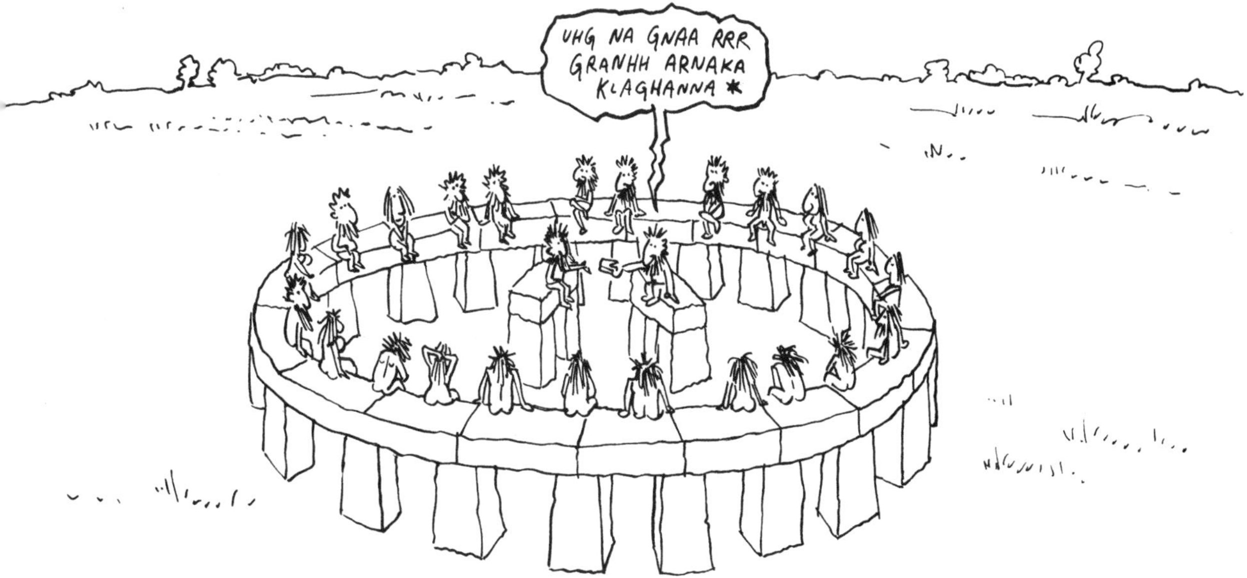
UHG NA GNAA RRR GRANHH ARNAKA KLAGHANNA *

* "YOU'VE GOT THIRTY-TWO THOUSAND FLINT ARROWHEADS - BUT I'D LOVE TO GIVE YOU THIS PROMISSORY TABLET FOR SIXTY-FOUR THOUSAND"

POST BOXES, KEENLY AWARE OF THEIR HIGHER STATUS, TAUNT LITTER BINS WHEN WE'RE NOT AROUND

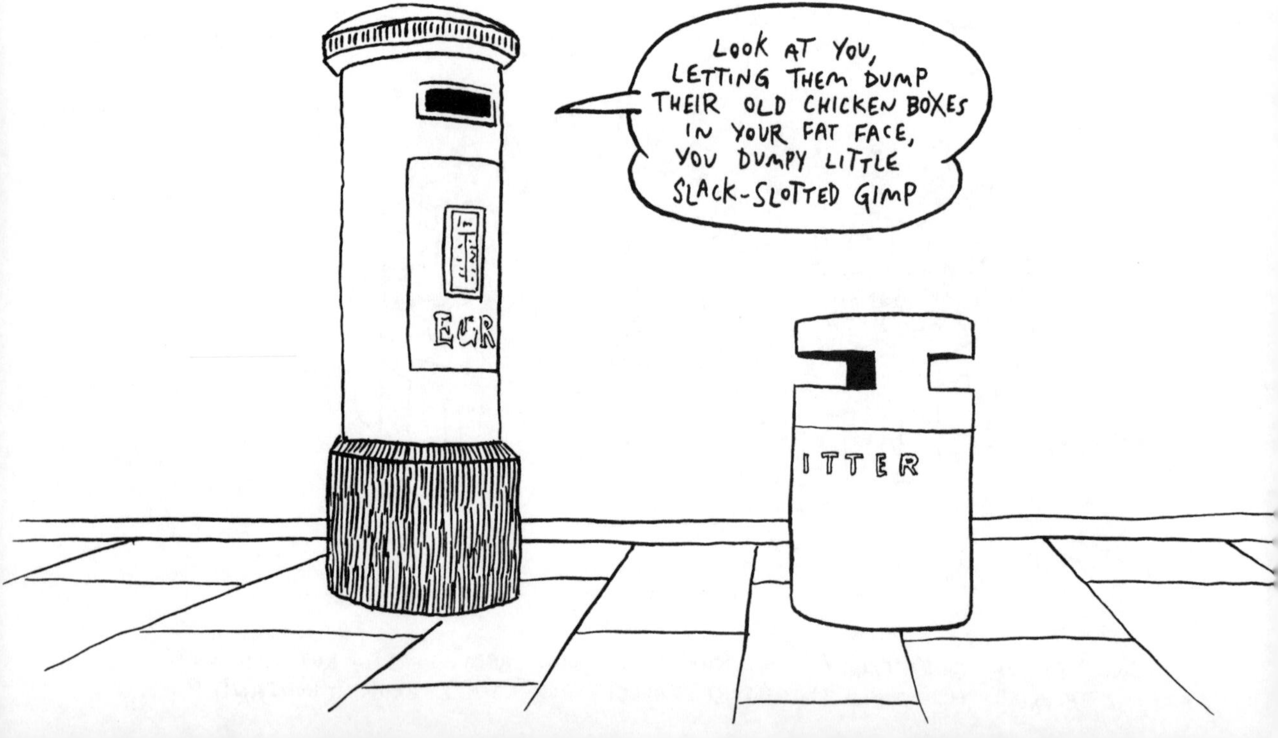
LOOK AT YOU, LETTING THEM DUMP THEIR OLD CHICKEN BOXES IN YOUR FAT FACE, YOU DUMPY LITTLE SLACK-SLOTTED GIMP
ITTER

DON'T BOTHER THROWING
BREAD AT THE DUCKS

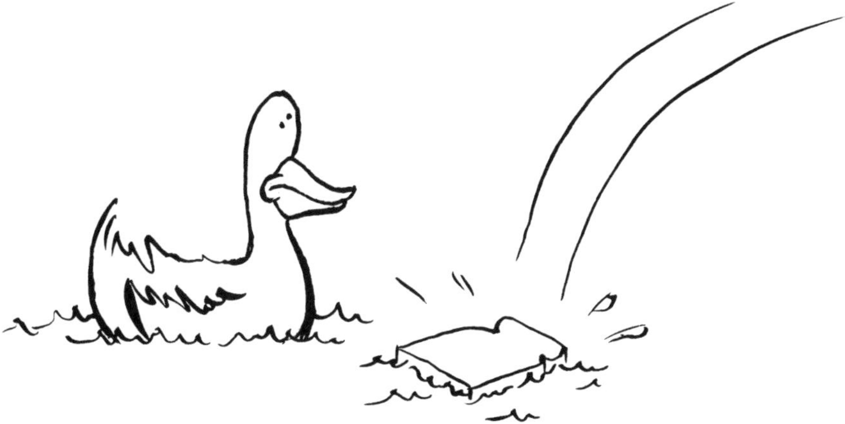

THEY'VE ALL
GONE ATKINS

DUE TO POST-WAR PLASTIC SHORTAGES THE
VERY FIRST BARBIE DOLLS WERE MADE OF
WOOD WITH MONKEY SKULLS FOR HEADS

you type the word 'Google' into Google

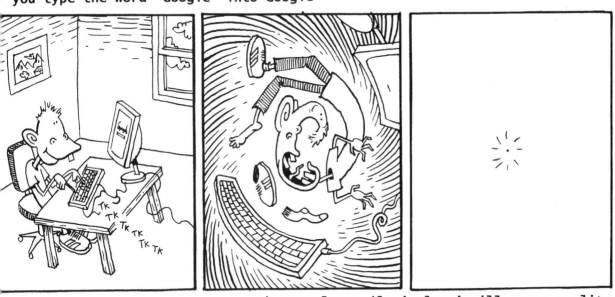

the resultant 'logic loop' will cause reality
to fold in on itself and the universe will
collapse into an infinitely dense dot

IF ANYONE SIGNS
THAT PLASTER CAST
THE INK WILL
GO THROUGH AND
TATTOO YOUR
ARM

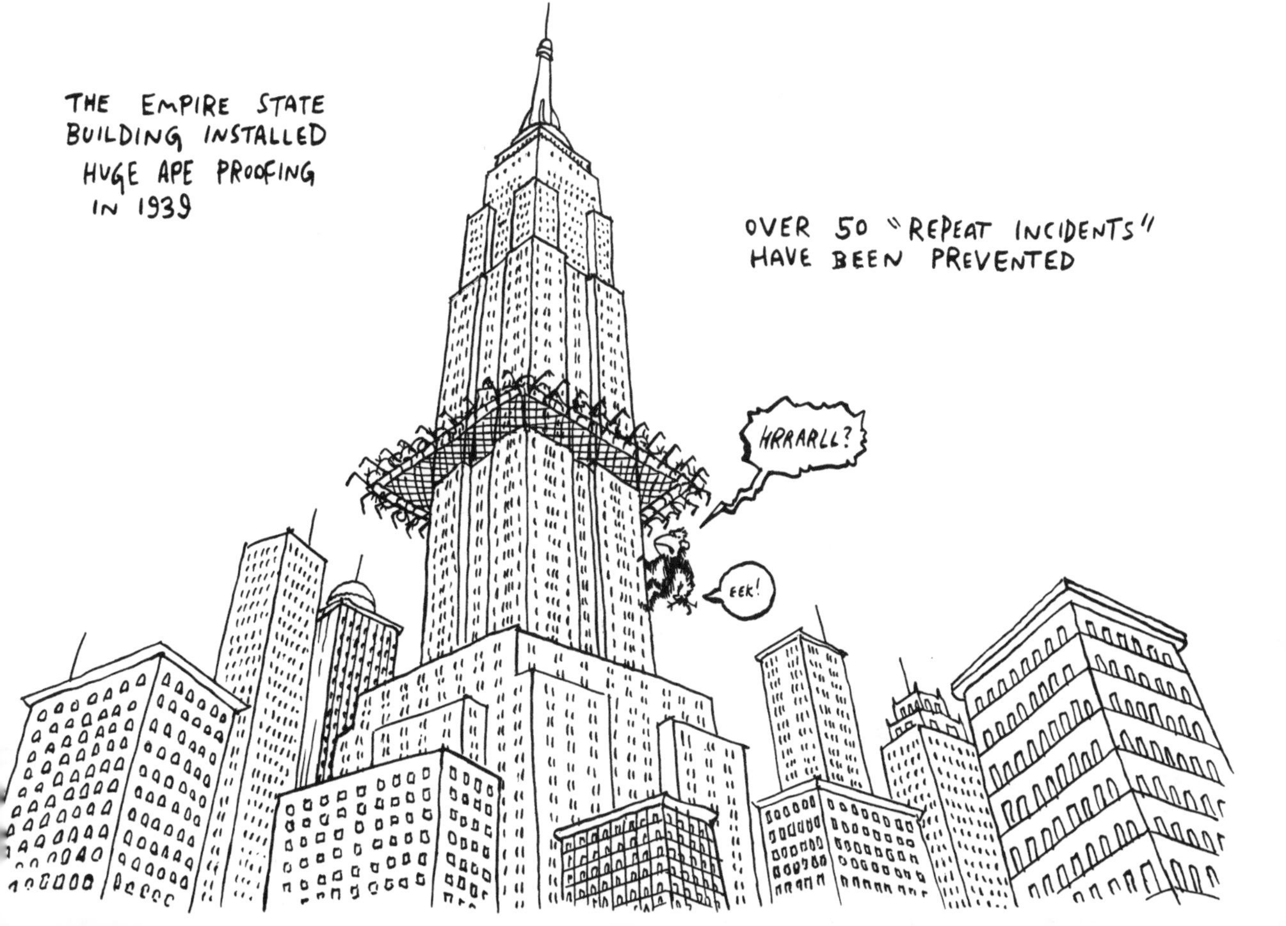
THE EMPIRE STATE BUILDING INSTALLED HUGE APE PROOFING IN 1939
OVER 50 "REPEAT INCIDENTS" HAVE BEEN PREVENTED
HRRARLL?
EEK!

your suitcases don't travel on the plane with you

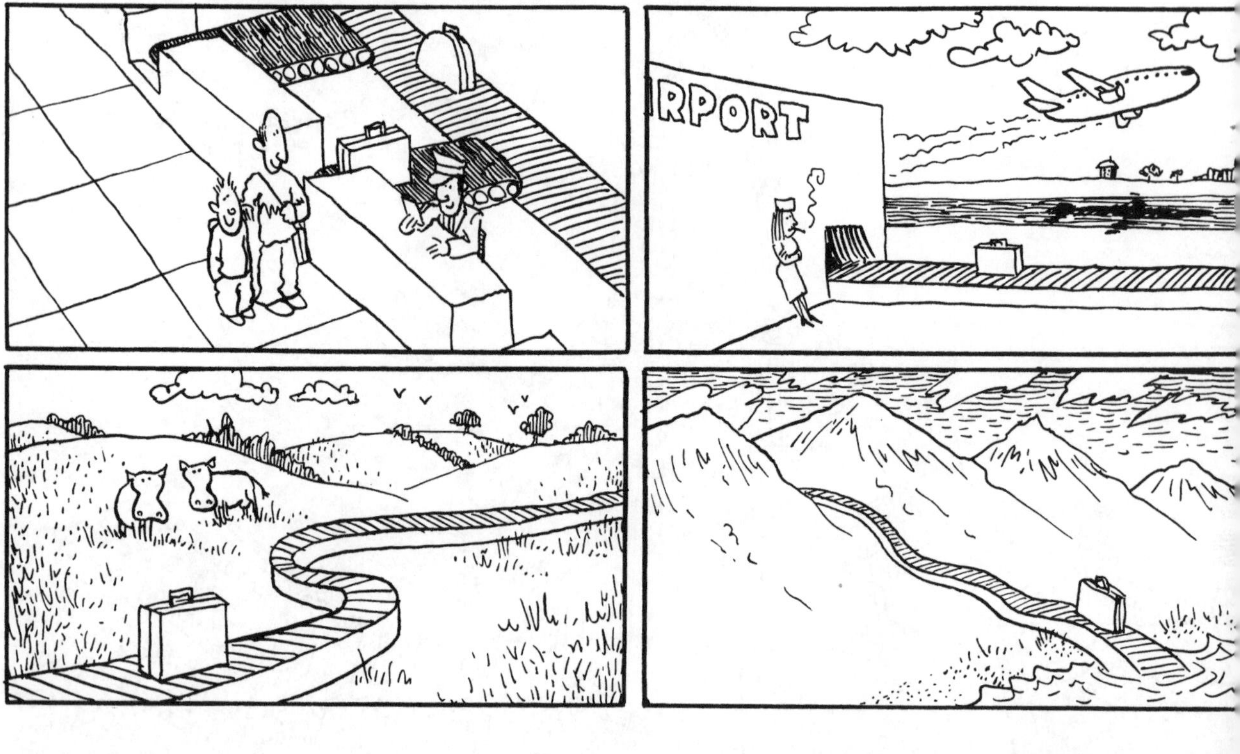
RPORT

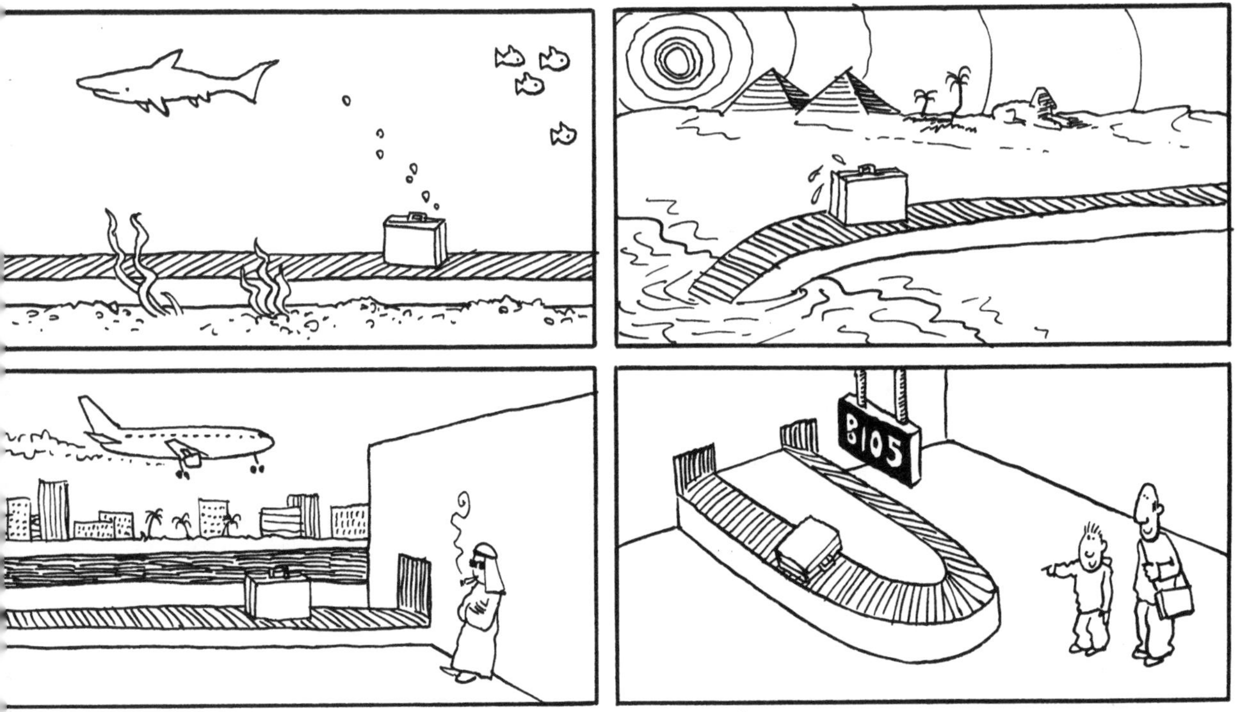
B105

they go the whole way by carousel

WHEN SUNLIGHT STRIKES
THE STEAM ABOVE A MUG
OF BOVRIL

YOU'LL SEE A
BROWN RAINBOW

the last winter olympics weren't very popular so they're going to start having the autumn olympics instead

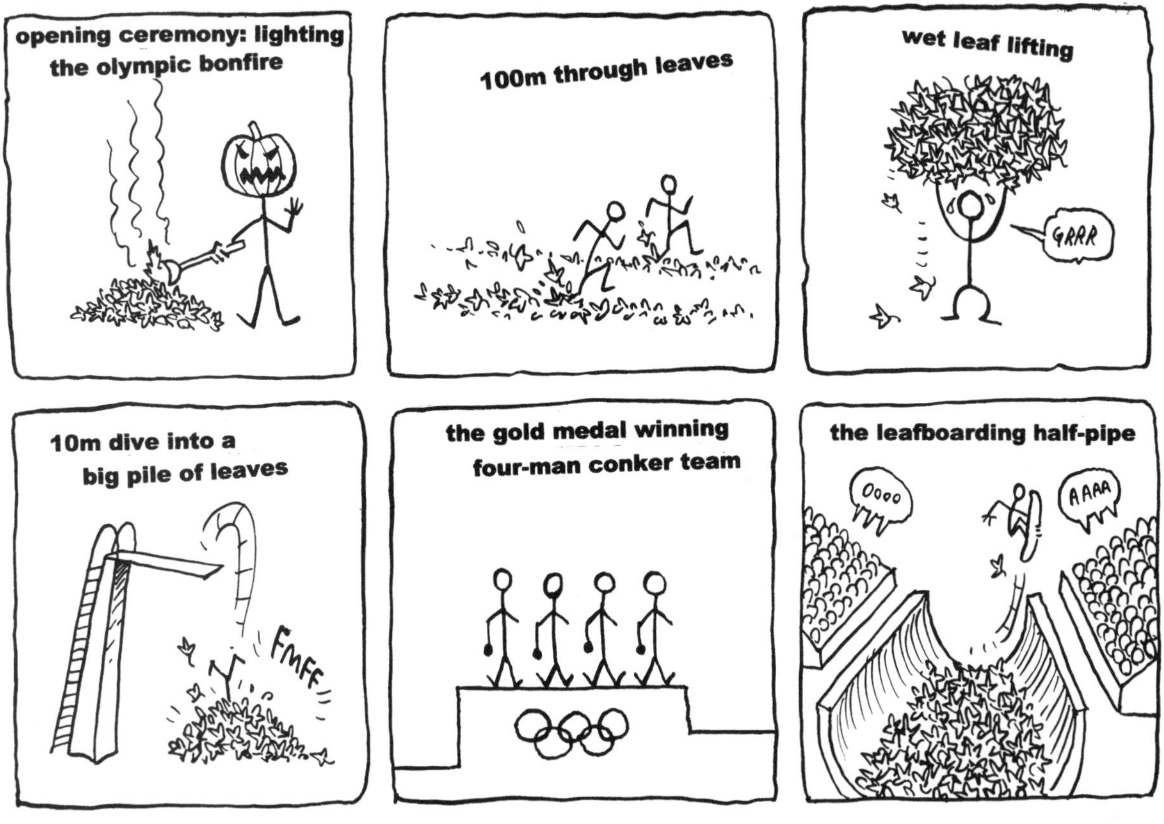
opening ceremony: lighting the olympic bonfire
100m through leaves
wet leaf lifting
GRRR
10m dive into a big pile of leaves
FMFF
the gold medal winning four-man conker team
the leafboarding half-pipe
Oooo
AAAA

THE GREAT WALL OF CHINA HAS A CAT FLAP EVERY FIVE MILES

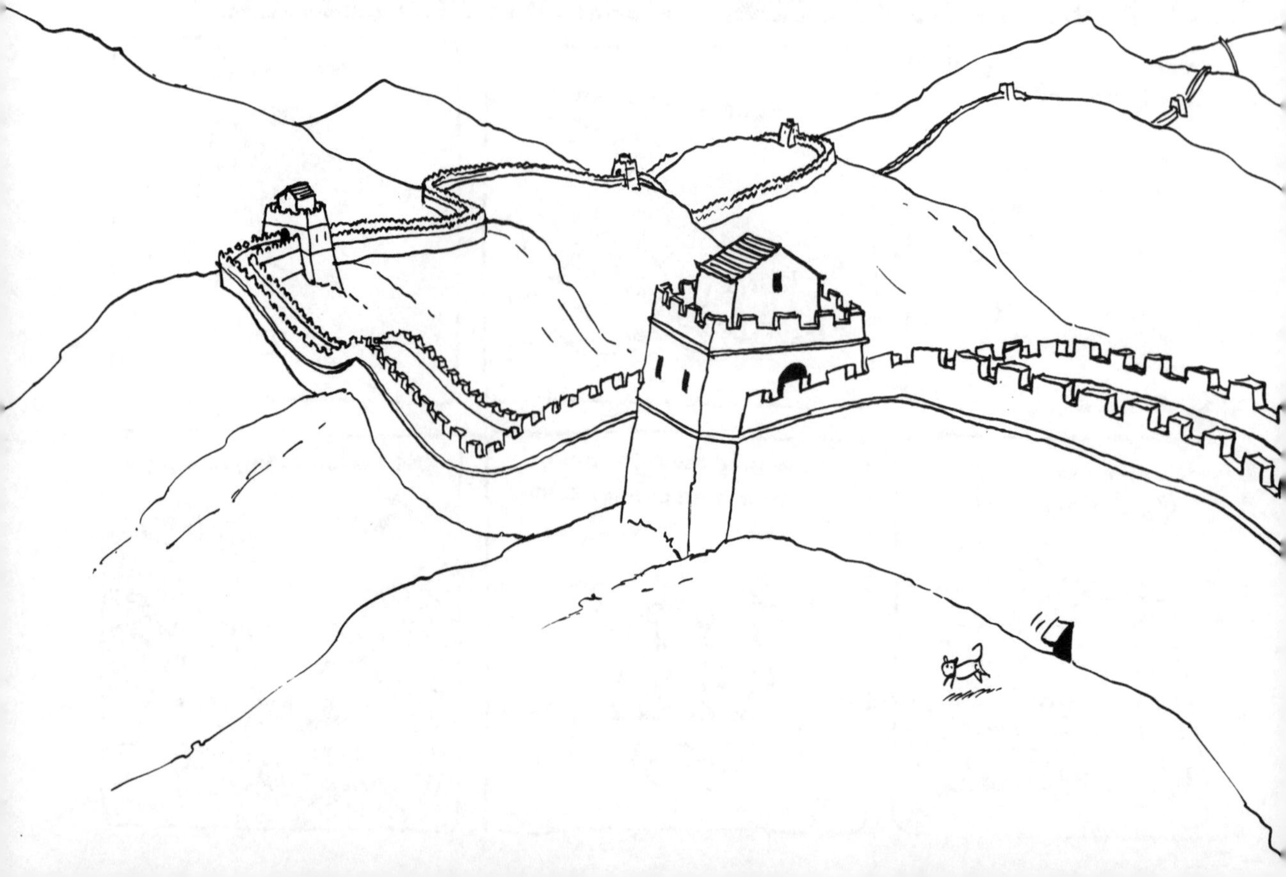

dead people are just being lazy

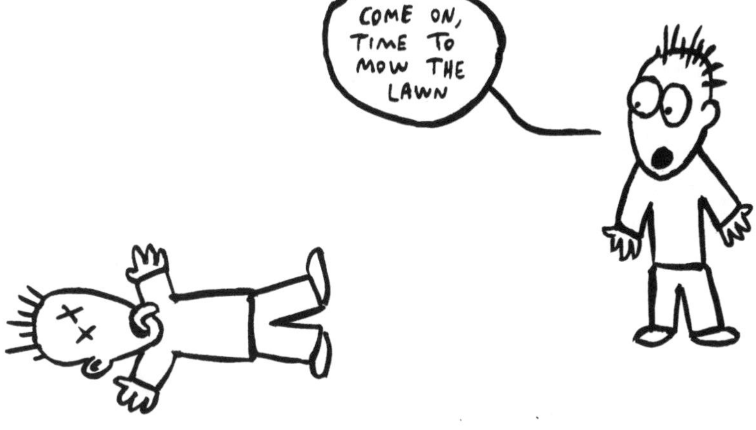
COME ON, TIME TO MOW THE LAWN

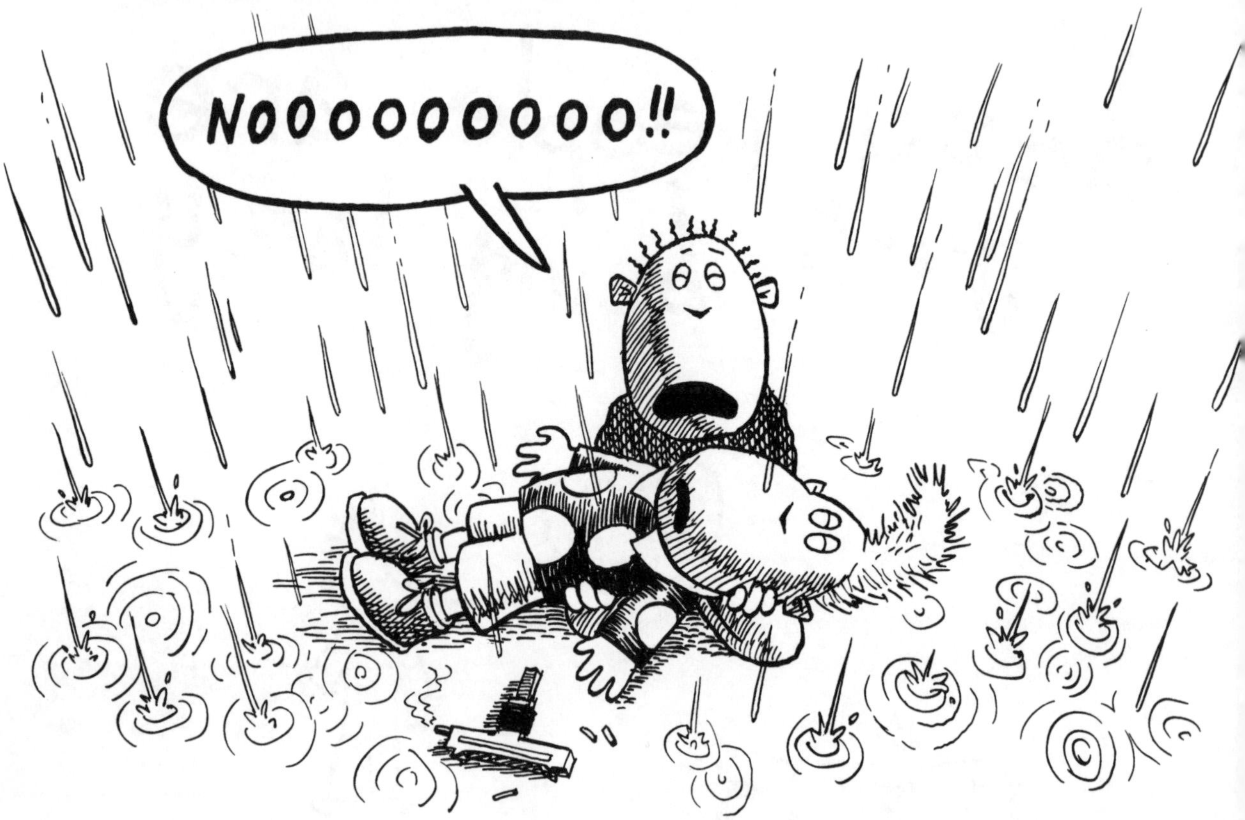
NOOOOOOOOOO!!

THE VERY LAST EPISODE OF THE TWEENIES ENDS IN A MASSIVE SHOOT-OUT THEN THEY ROLL THE CREDITS SILENTLY OVER BLACK

DROP A TOOTH
IN A GLASS OF
COKE

AND AFTER
A DAY

IT BECOMES
A WHITE
BUTTERFLY

FIRST CLASS SEATS ARE ALWAYS AT THE FRONT OF THE PLANE BECAUSE BUSINESSMEN NEED TO GET TO PLACES *ONE SECOND SOONER* THAN EVERYONE ELSE

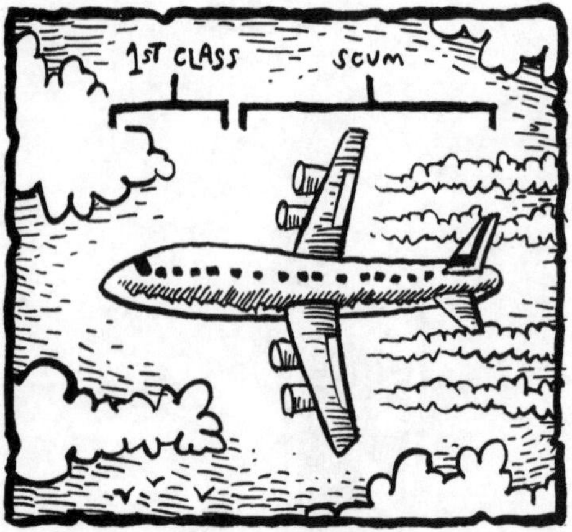
1ST CLASS
SCUM

THEIR TIME IS *THAT* PRECIOUS

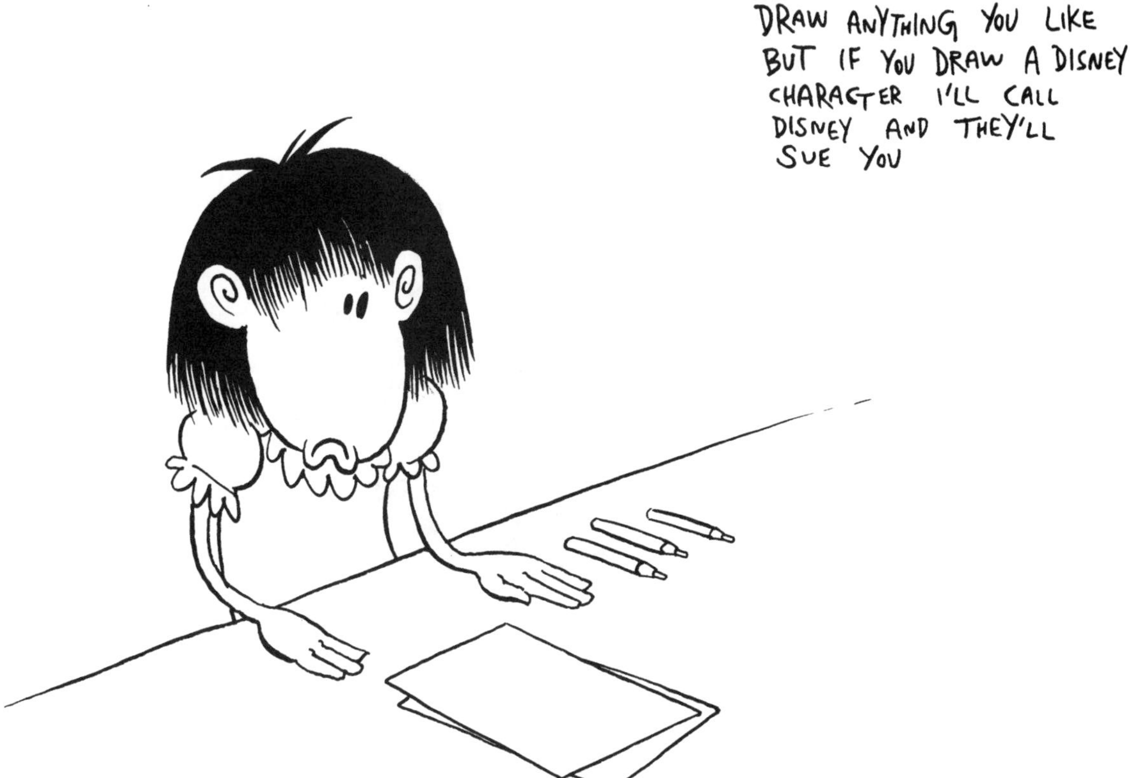
DRAW ANYTHING YOU LIKE BUT IF YOU DRAW A DISNEY CHARACTER I'LL CALL DISNEY AND THEY'LL SUE YOU

On St. Patrick's Day every Irish family has a whole roast leprechaun

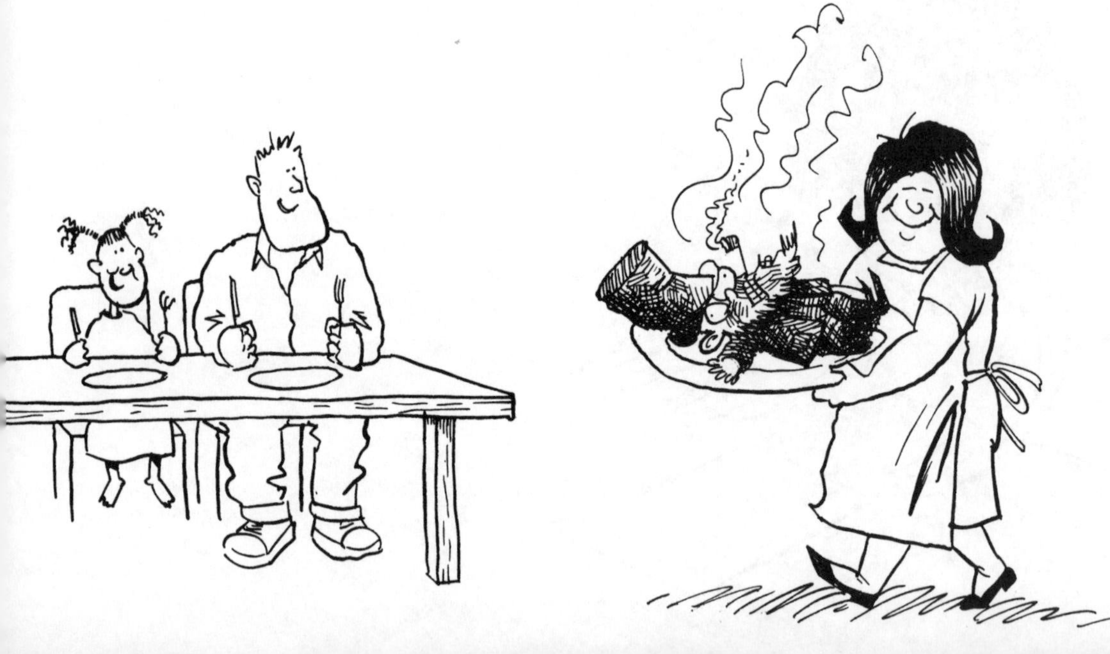

shove uncooked spaghetti down the little holes in the phone receiver

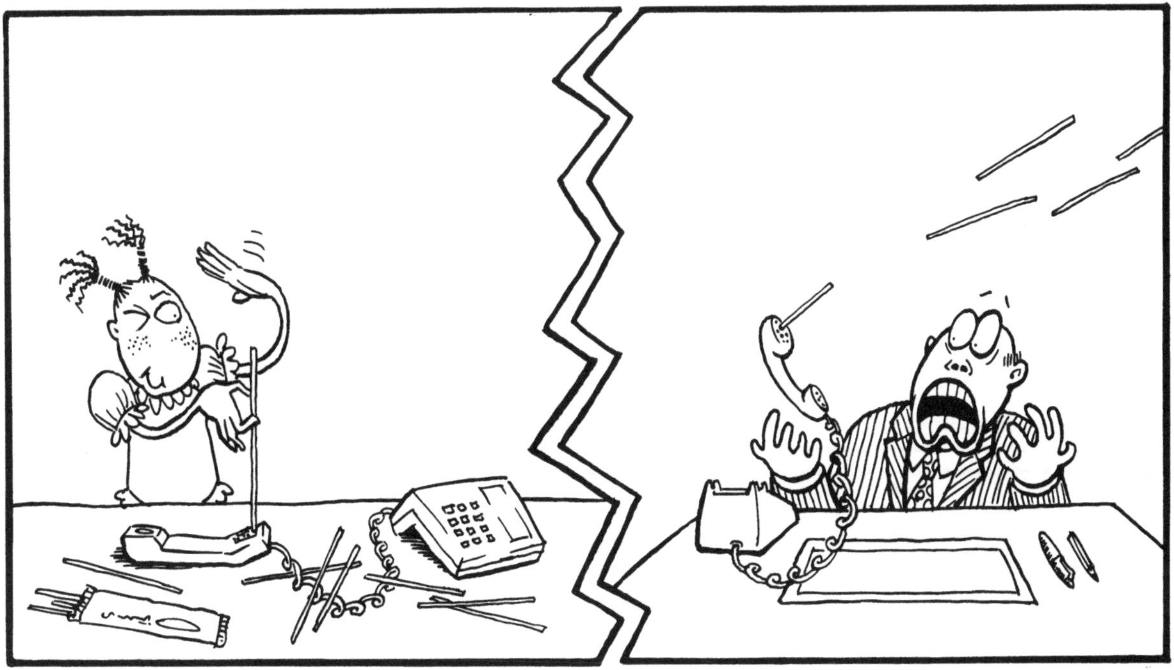

it'll shoot out in your friend's ear

SNAILS LIKE TO PLAY 'CHICKEN'

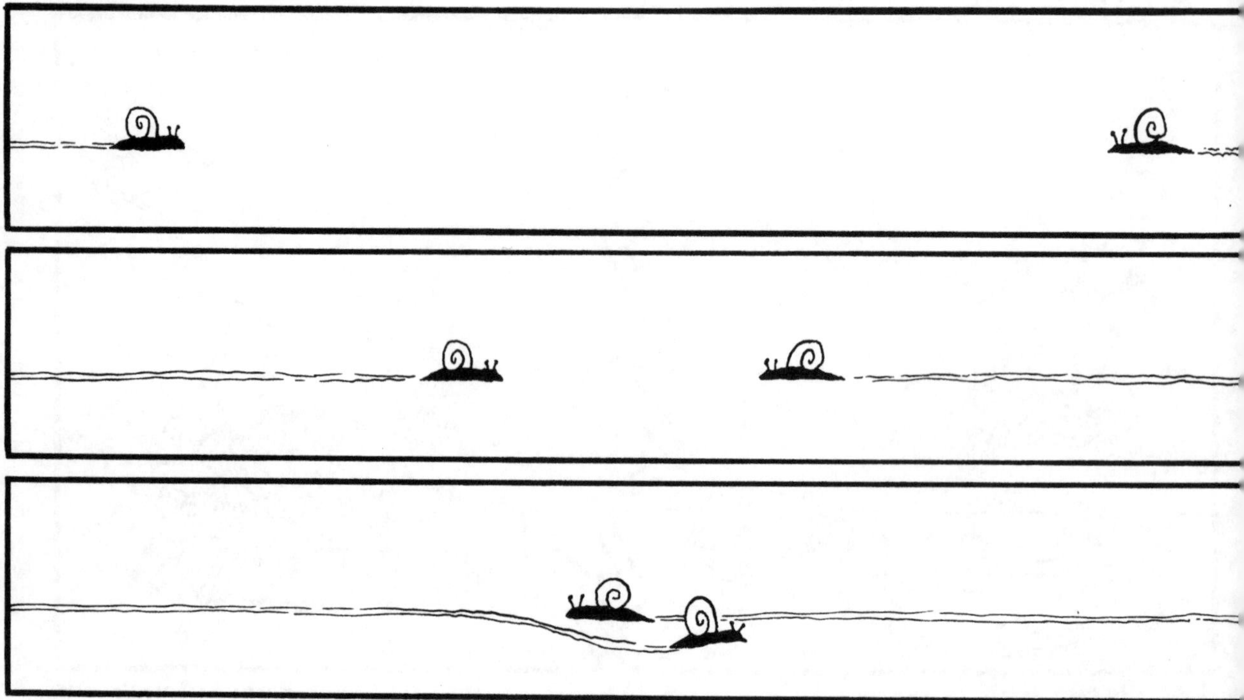

IT TAKES THEM 2½ HOURS

IN 1994 BRANDING CONSULTANTS GAVE JESUS SHADES AND A SNOWBOARD TO MAKE HIM LOOK "COOL"

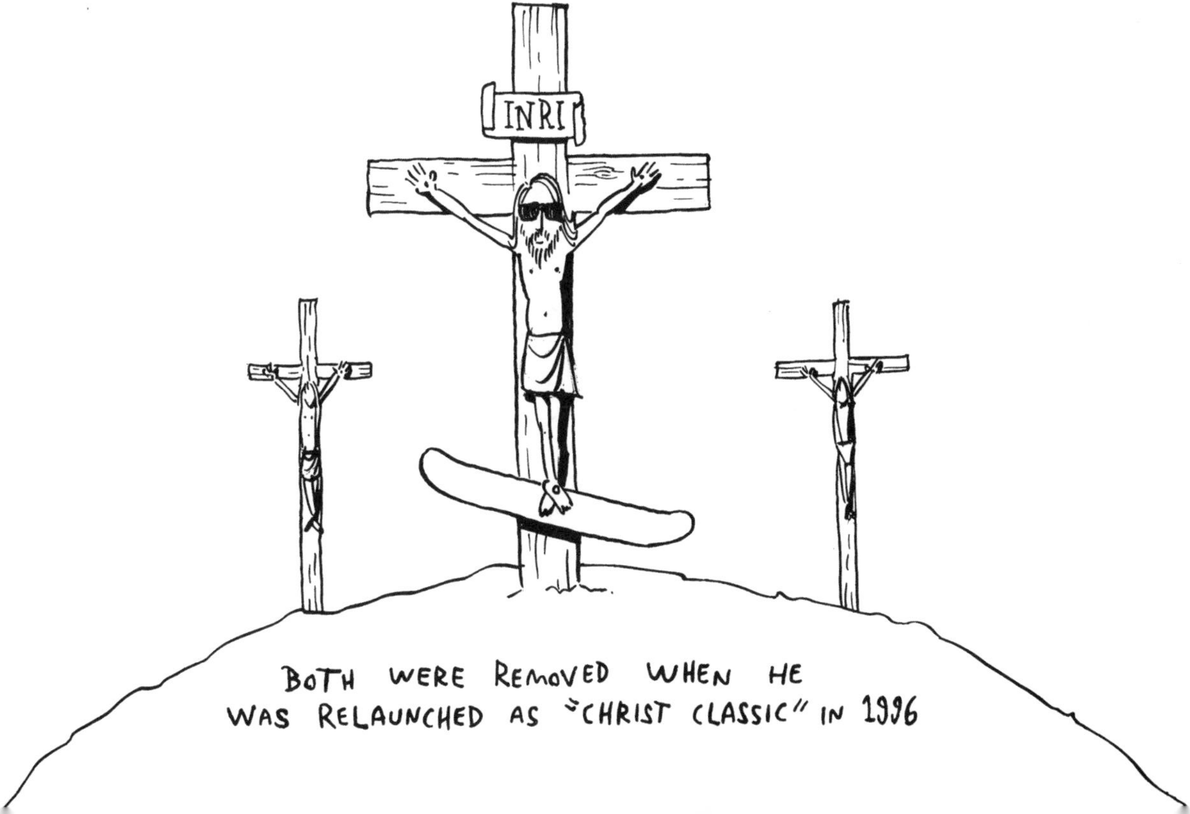
INRI
BOTH WERE REMOVED WHEN HE WAS RELAUNCHED AS "CHRIST CLASSIC" IN 1996

BOWLING BALLS HAVE RETRACTABLE EYES

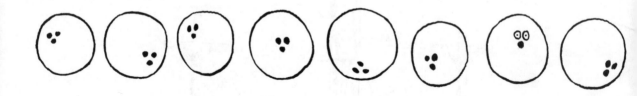

IN 1942 HITLER TOOK A CAREER BREAK TO GO BACKPACKING

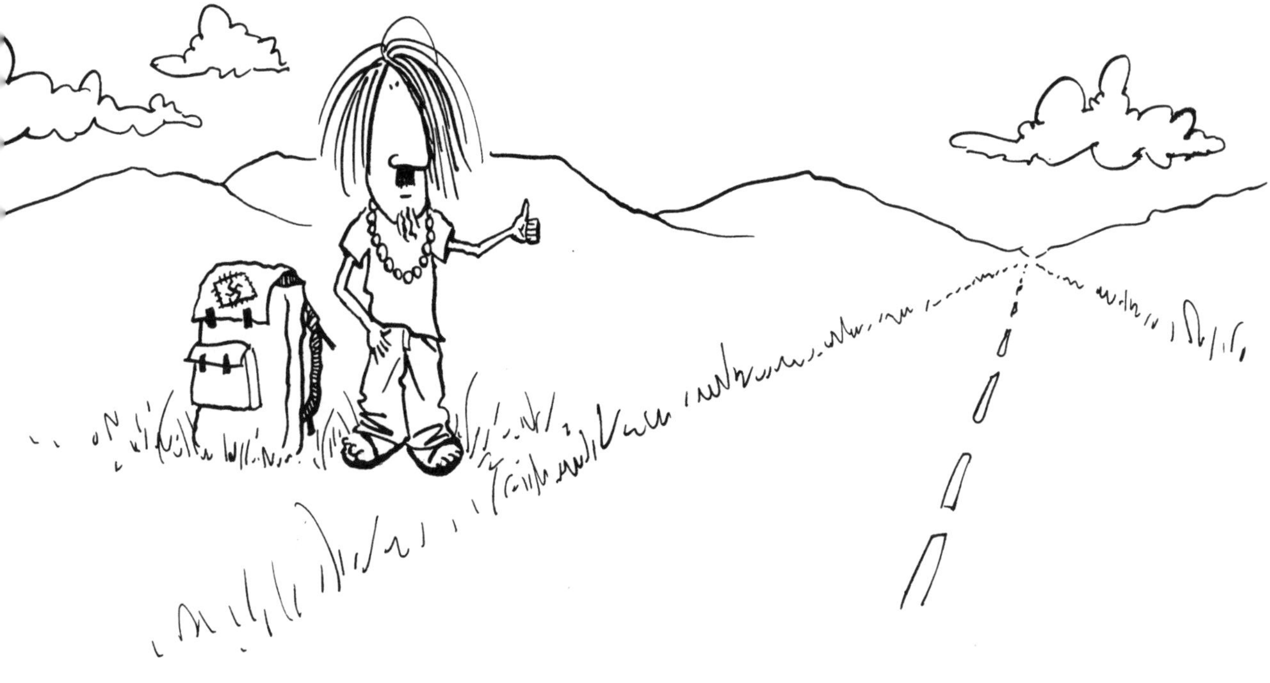

A LITTLE-KNOWN RULE OF TENNIS SAYS YOU
CAN THROW YOUR OWN POO AT THE OTHER
PLAYER WHILE THEY ARE SERVING

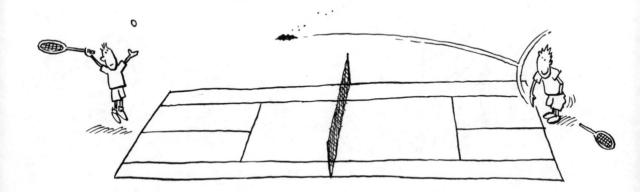

SHAGGY DIED IN
THE VIETNAM WAR

EVERY YEAR SCOOBY
PLACES A VERY TALL
SANDWICH ON HIS
GRAVE

PENGUINS ARE JUST
PRETENDING THEY CAN'T FLY

IF YOU THROW ONE OFF
A TALL BUILDING YOU'LL
SEE FOR YOURSELF

The Earth's steering wheel is located at the North Pole. It is manned by the 'Earth Driver'.

He steers us on one circuit of the sun every 365 days. If he turns a fraction too much to the left, the sun's gravity pulls us in and we die by fire. A fraction too much to the right and we spin off into the void of space and freeze to death.

The Earth Driver must never, ever fall asleep.

Polar explorers bring him flasks of coffee.

THE WORLD'S TALLEST DWARF IS
HERNAN DOMINGO OF BILBAO

HE IS SIX FOOT TWO INCHES TALL

THE HUNGRY HUNGRY HIPPOS HAVE JOINED WEIGHT WATCHERS

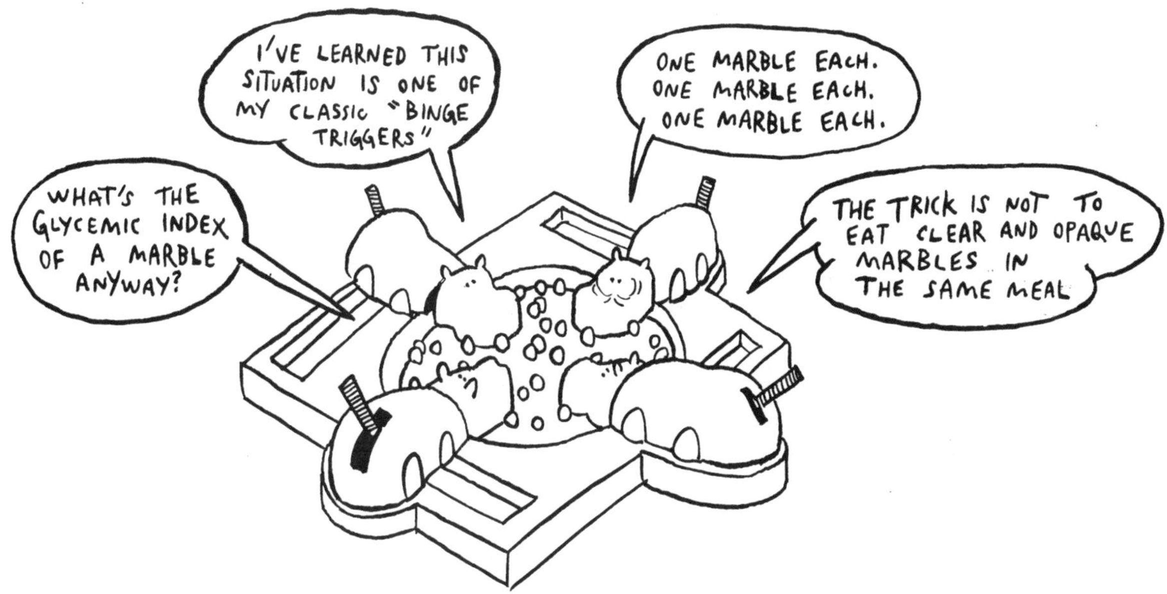
WHAT'S THE GLYCEMIC INDEX OF A MARBLE ANYWAY?
I'VE LEARNED THIS SITUATION IS ONE OF MY CLASSIC "BINGE TRIGGERS"
ONE MARBLE EACH. ONE MARBLE EACH. ONE MARBLE EACH.
THE TRICK IS NOT TO EAT CLEAR AND OPAQUE MARBLES IN THE SAME MEAL

YOU'VE JUST GOT TO TRY

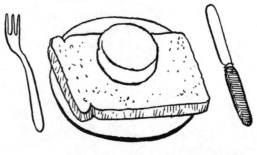

IT'S DELICIOUS!

URINAL CAKE ON TOAST

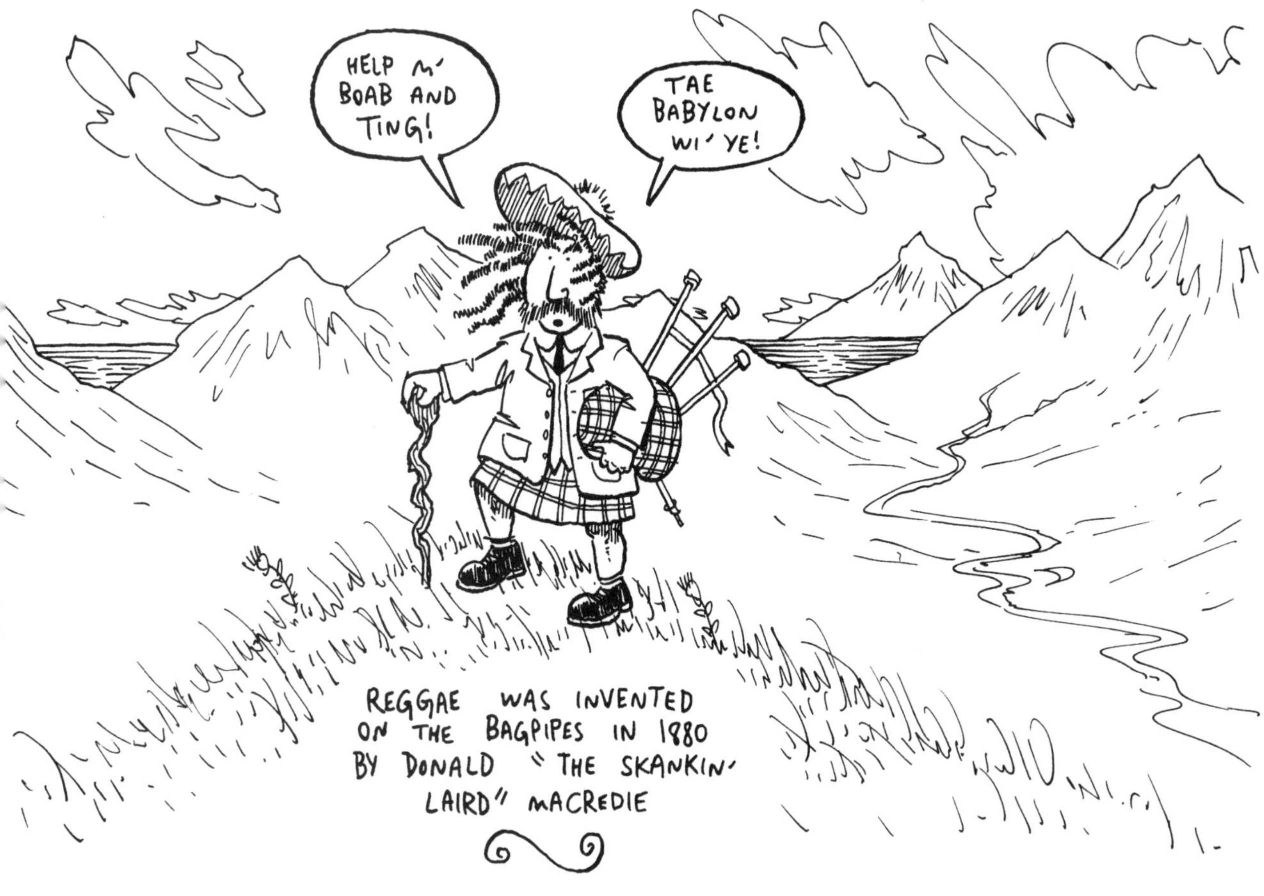
HELP M' BOAB AND TING!
TAE BABYLON WI' YE!
REGGAE WAS INVENTED ON THE BAGPIPES IN 1880 BY DONALD "THE SKANKIN' LAIRD" MACREDIE

Heaven isn't full but its car park is

Since 1991 blessed souls have been driving round looking for a space

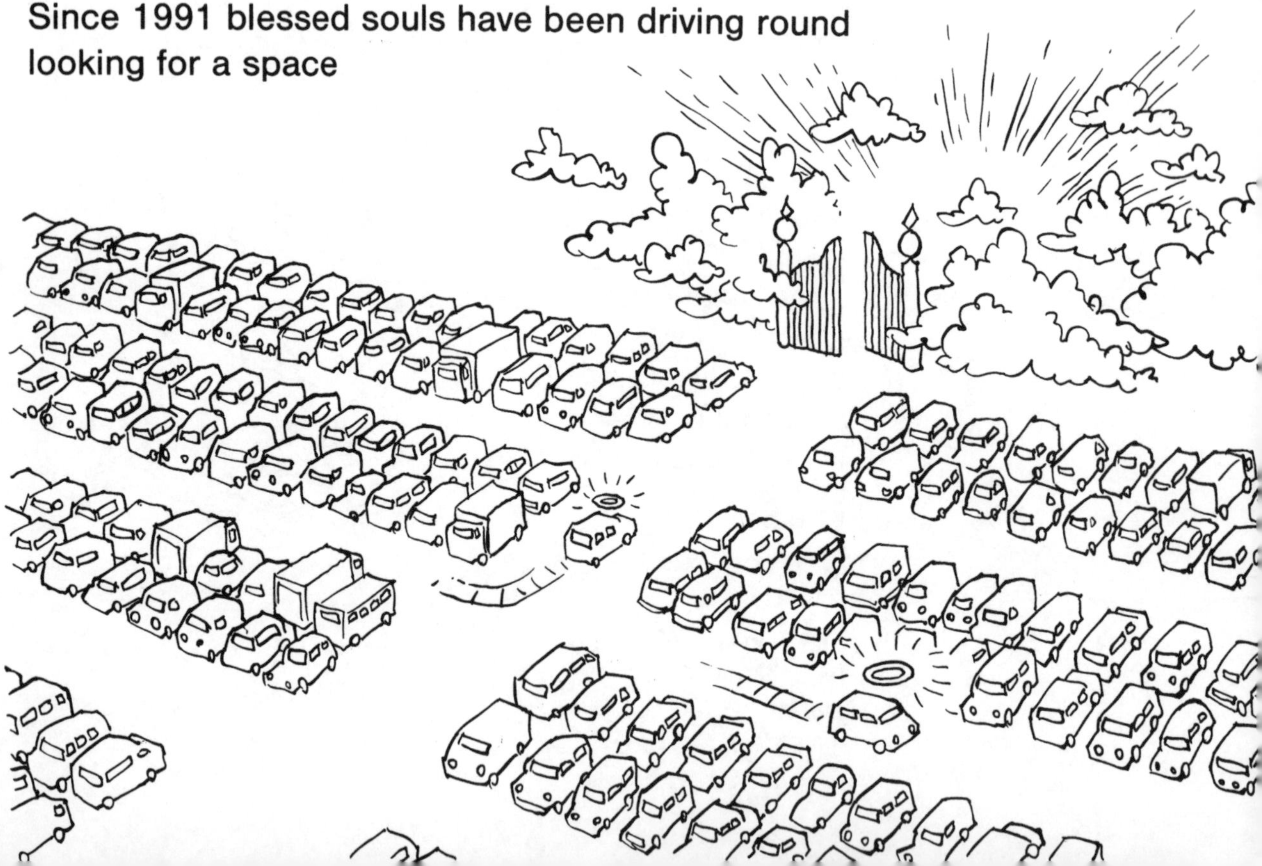

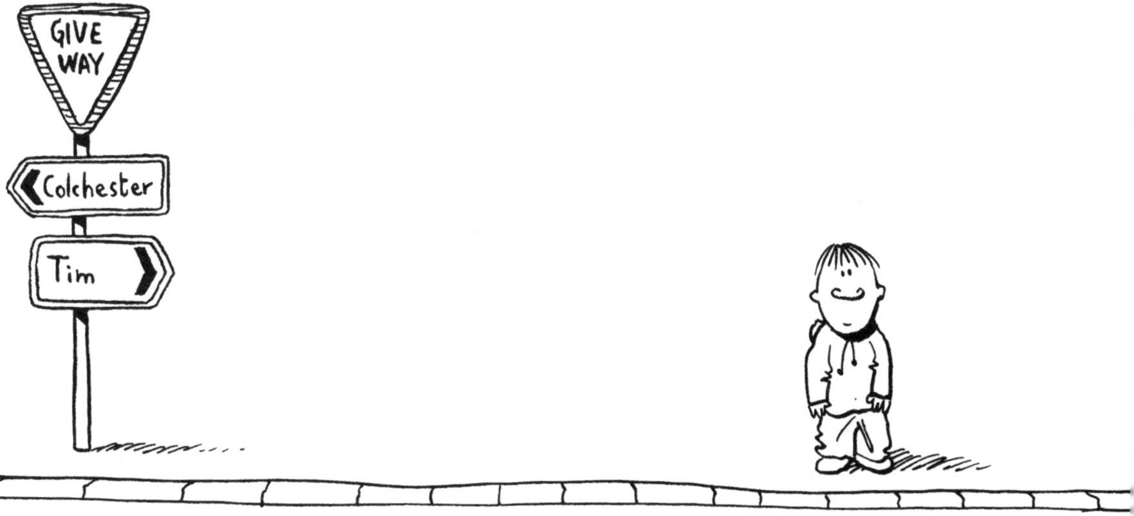
GIVE
WAY
Colchester
Tim

IF YOU STAND STILL LONG ENOUGH THE GOVERNMENT WILL PUT UP ROAD SIGNS POINTING TOWARDS YOU

UNCLE PAUL HAS A ZIP WHERE HIS BUMHOLE
SHOULD BE BUT YOU CAN'T EVER MENTION IT TO HIM

WATCH OUT FOR

THE BALL-PIT SHARK

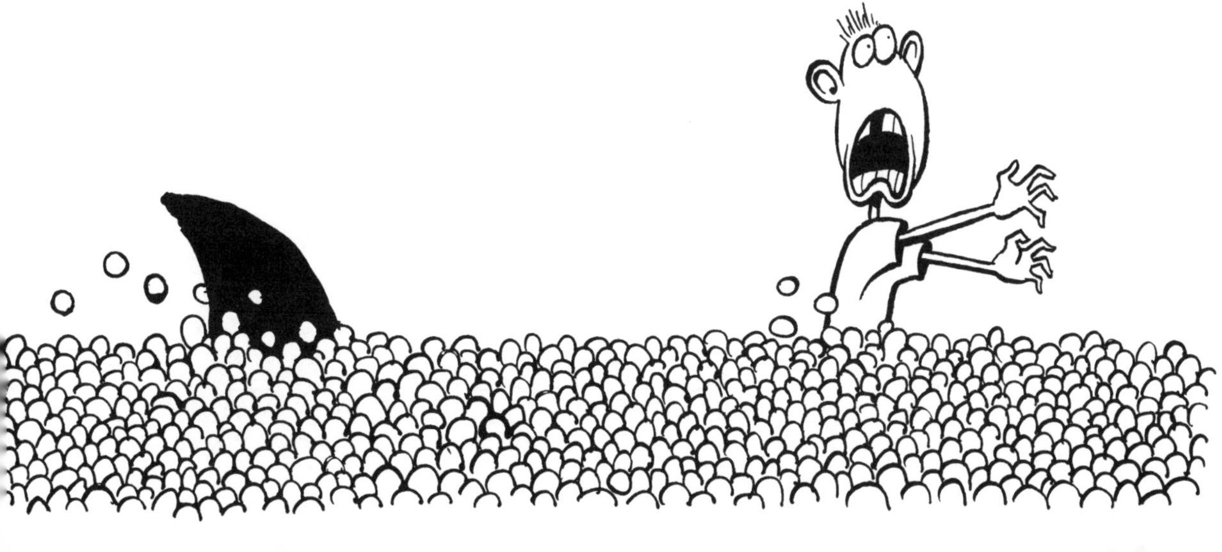

IF YOU WRITE ALL THE NUMBERS UP TO INFINITY I'LL GIVE YOU

INFINITY POUNDS

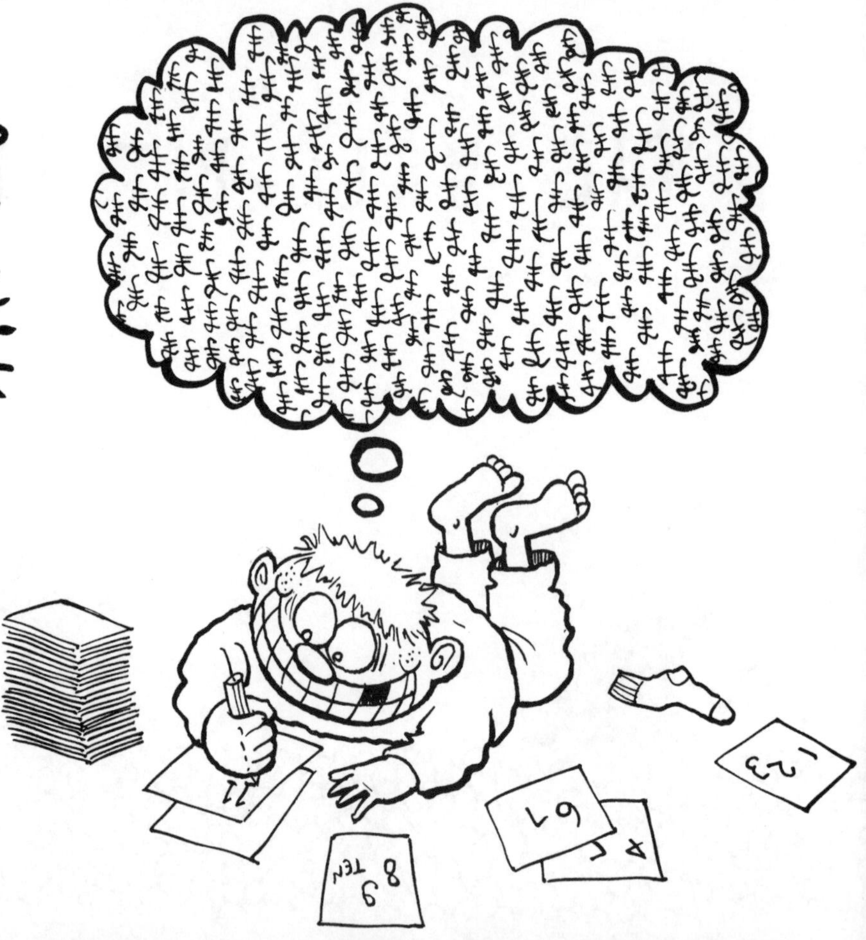

THE MOON IS CLOSER THAN YOU THINK

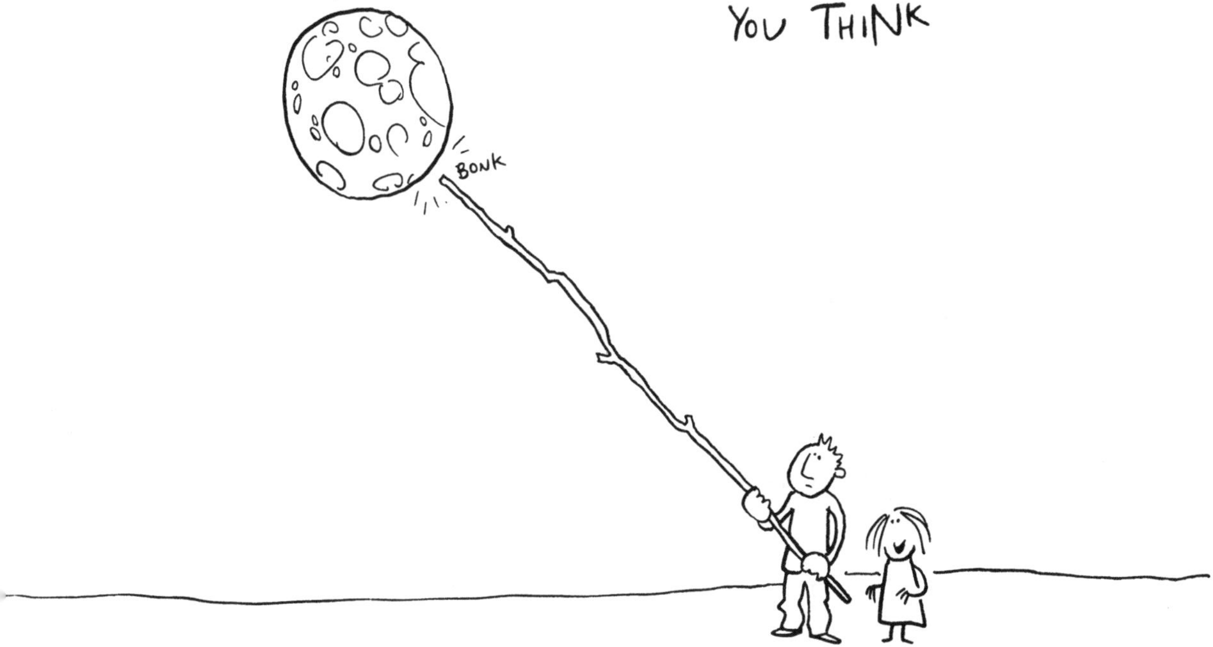
BONK

- GO TO INTERNET EXPLORER AND CLICK "REFRESH"
- THE COMPUTER WILL SQUIRT 7-UP INTO YOUR MOUTH

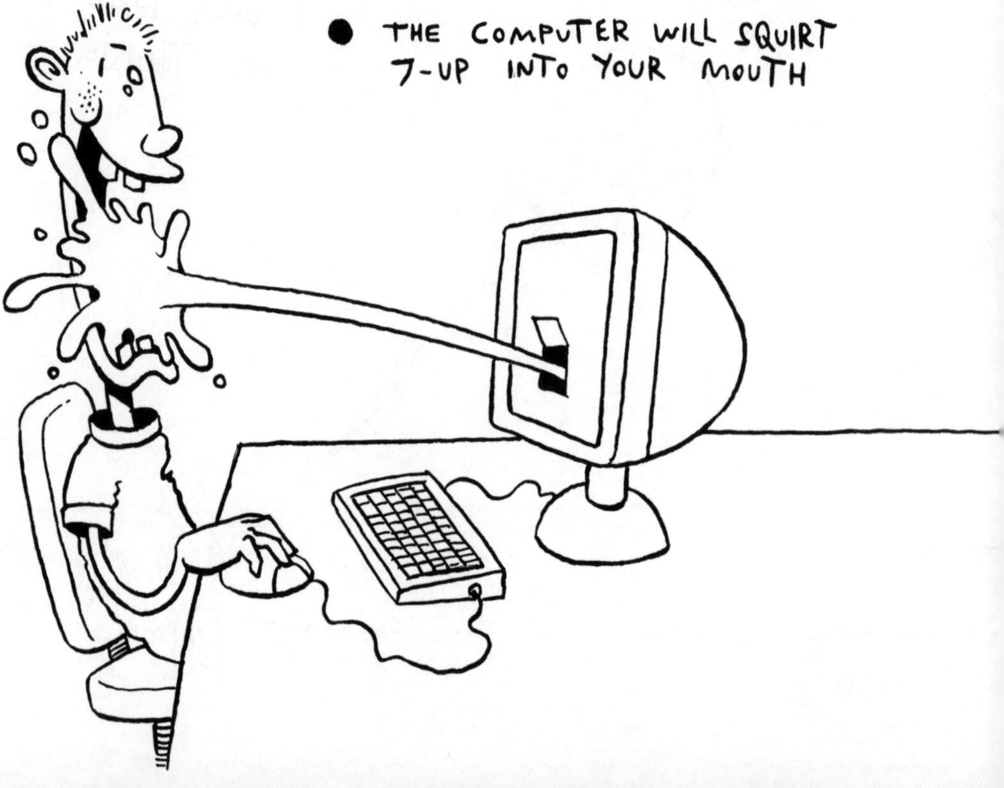

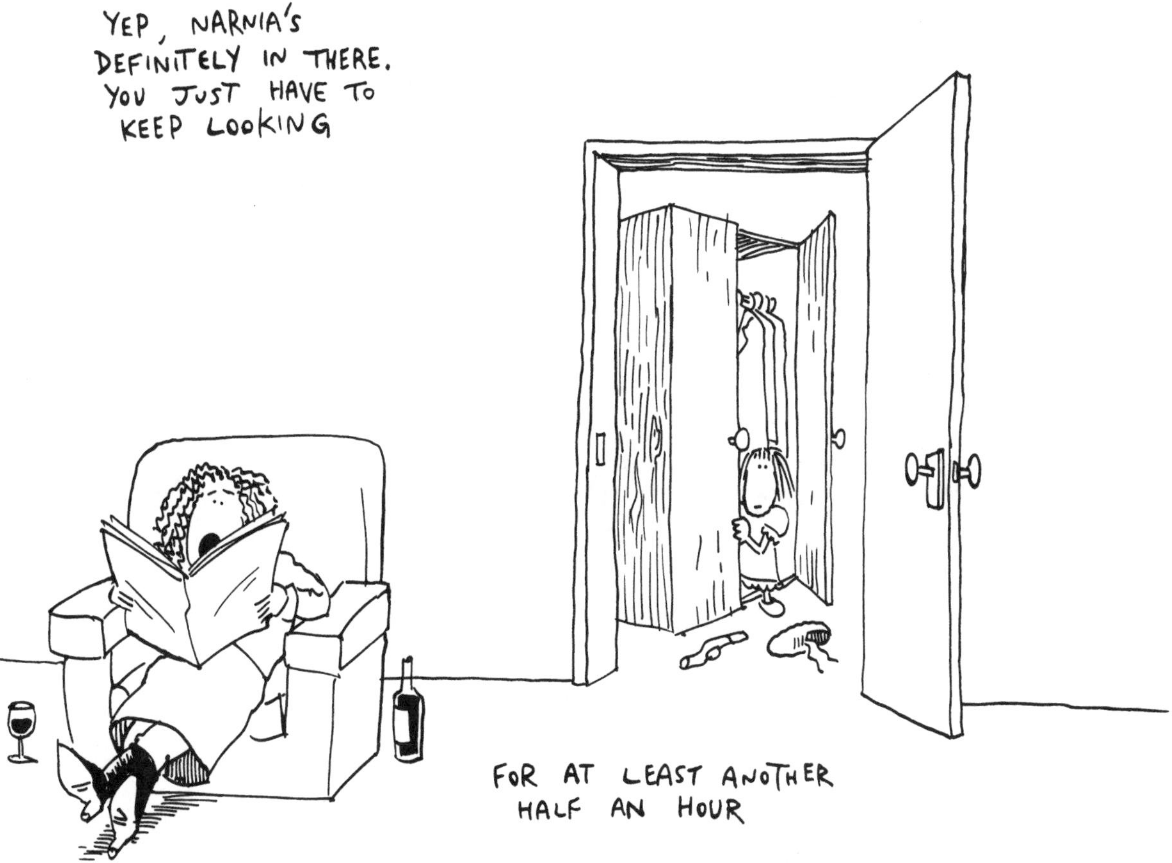
YEP, NARNIA'S DEFINITELY IN THERE. YOU JUST HAVE TO KEEP LOOKING
FOR AT LEAST ANOTHER HALF AN HOUR

if you swallow enough bubble gum
you can blow a massive bubble
from your arse

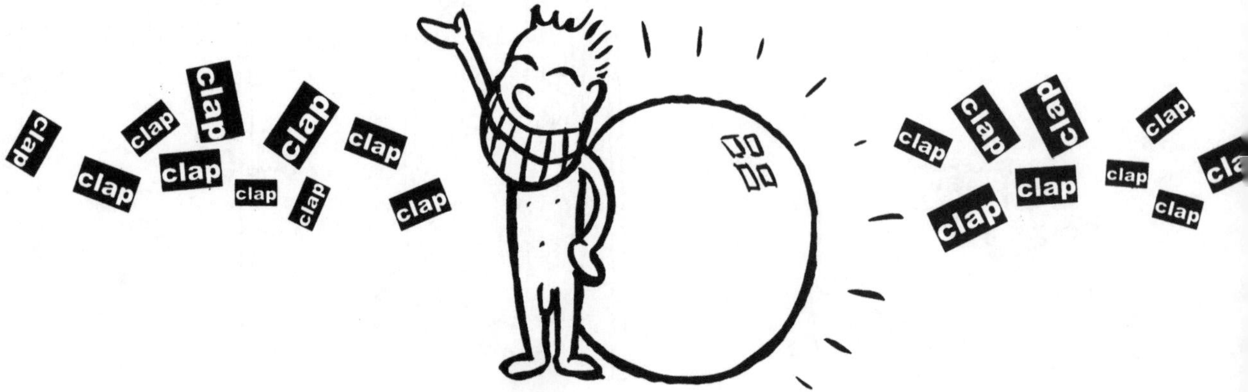
clap
clap
clap
clap
clap
clap
clap
clap
clap
clap
clap
clap
clap
clap
clap
clap
clap
clap

try it in school assembly

THE LAST WHEELED ELEPHANT WAS SHOT IN 1921

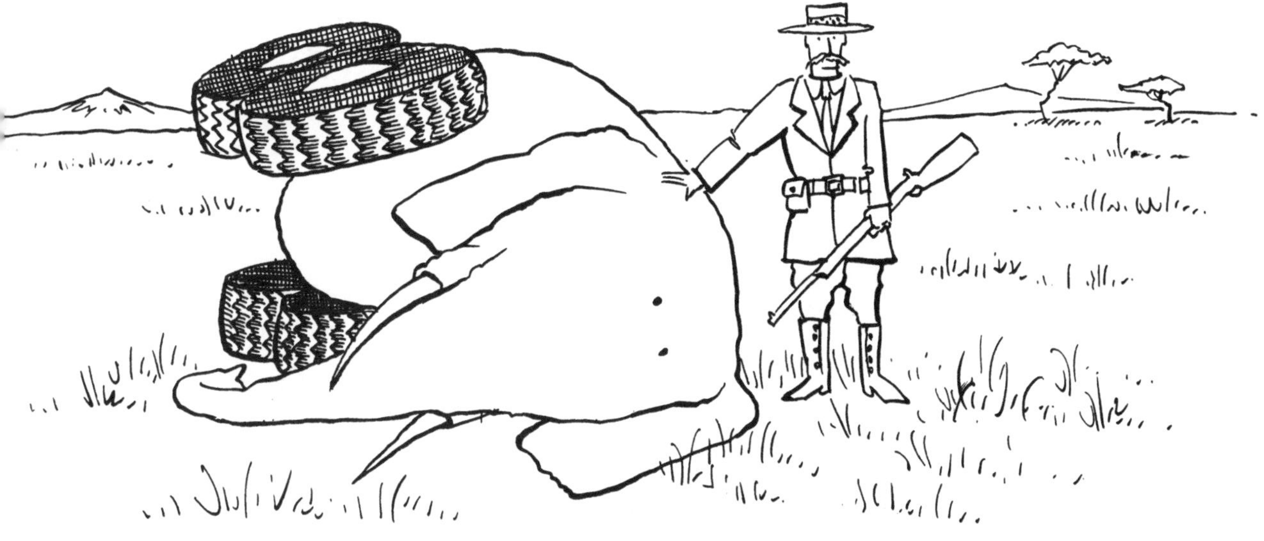

THERE WAS A SHORTAGE OF THE LETTER 'E'
DURING THE SECOND WORLD WAR

MOST GROWN-UPS WENT WITHOUT THEIR
RATION SO THAT THE KIDS COULD HAVE ENOUGH

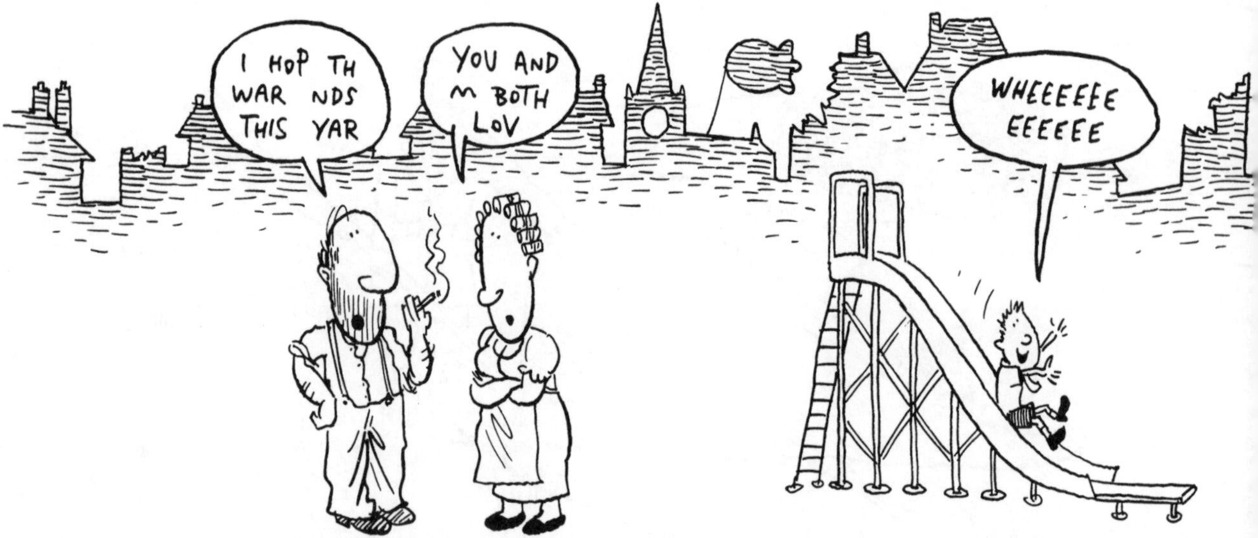
I HOP TH WAR NDS THIS YAR
YOU AND M BOTH LOV
WHEEEEEEE EEEEEE

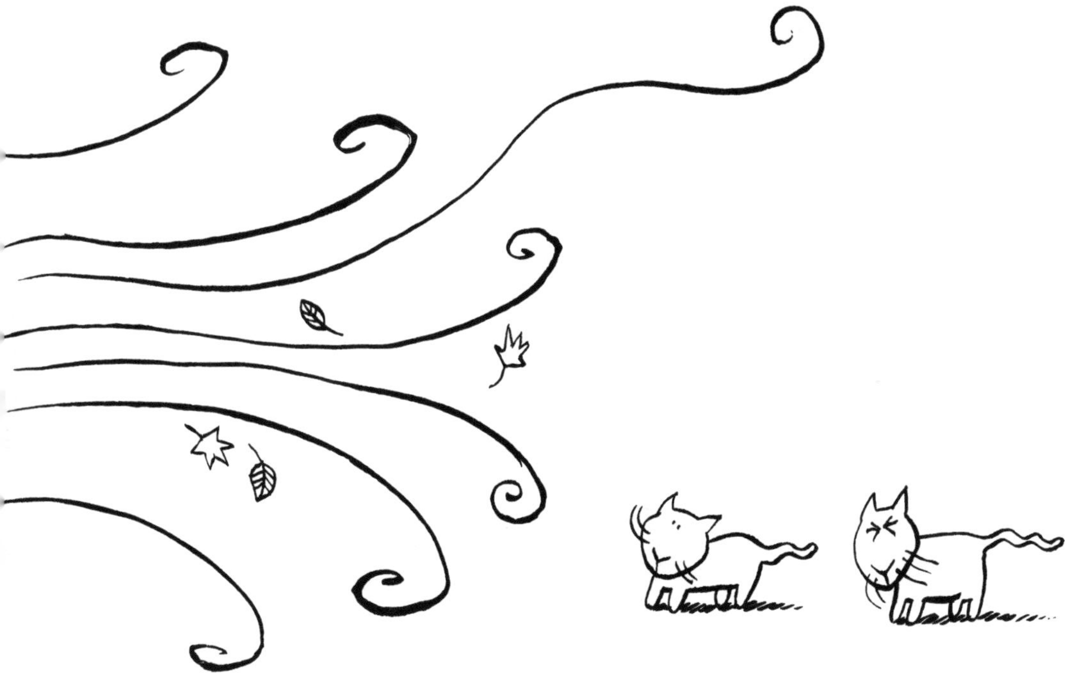

cats
can't
walk
into
the
wind

GOD LOOKS LIKE THIS

Nature File

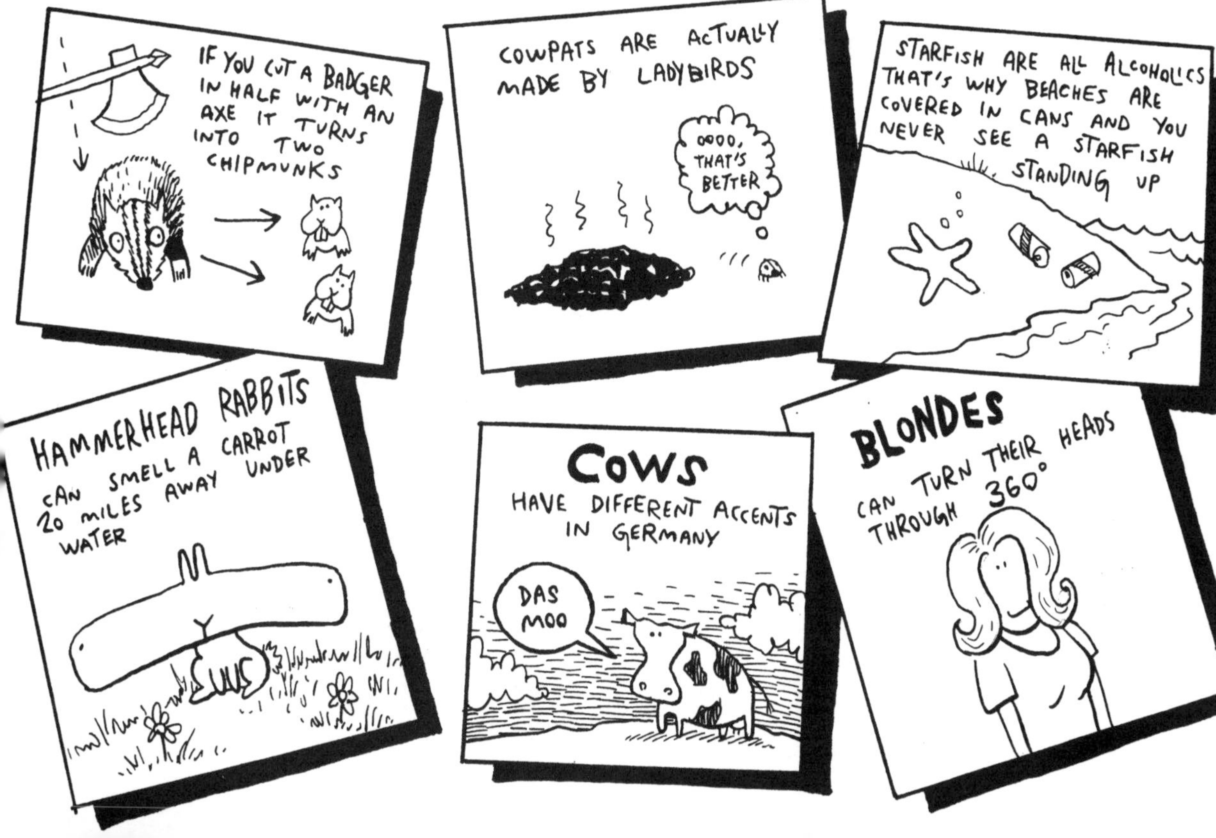
IF YOU CUT A BADGER IN HALF WITH AN AXE IT TURNS INTO TWO CHIPMUNKS
COWPATS ARE ACTUALLY MADE BY LADYBIRDS
OOOO, THAT'S BETTER
STARFISH ARE ALL ALCOHOLICS THAT'S WHY BEACHES ARE COVERED IN CANS AND YOU NEVER SEE A STARFISH STANDING UP
HAMMERHEAD RABBITS CAN SMELL A CARROT 20 MILES AWAY UNDER WATER
COWS HAVE DIFFERENT ACCENTS IN GERMANY
DAS MOO
BLONDES CAN TURN THEIR HEADS THROUGH 360°

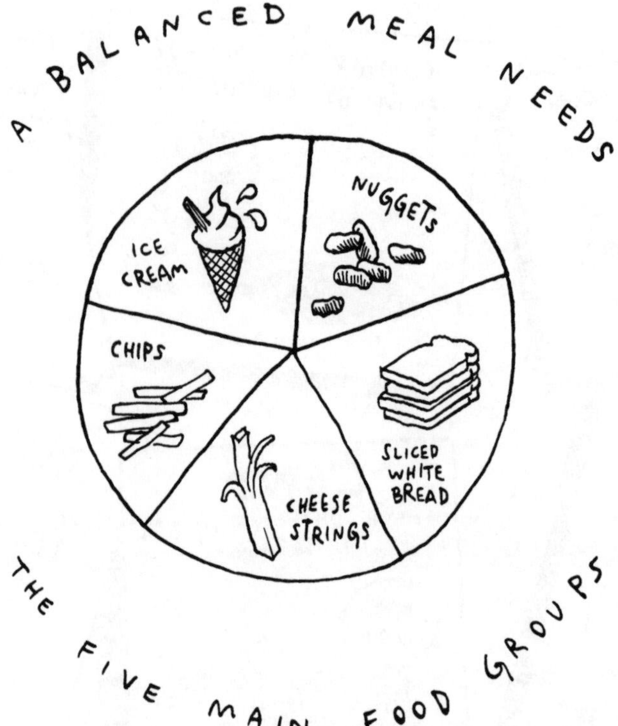
A BALANCED MEAL NEEDS
ICE CREAM
NUGGETS
CHIPS
SLICED WHITE BREAD
CHEESE STRINGS
THE FIVE MAIN FOOD GROUPS

IN ACTUAL FACT, ESKIMOS DON'T EVEN HAVE ONE WORD FOR SNOW
THAT STUFF'S FALLING AGAIN
WHAT STUFF?
UMM...
OH, YOU KNOW

AFTER 11 DAYS ON THE ARK NOAH GOT BORED AND KILLED ALL THE DINOSAURS FOR A LAUGH

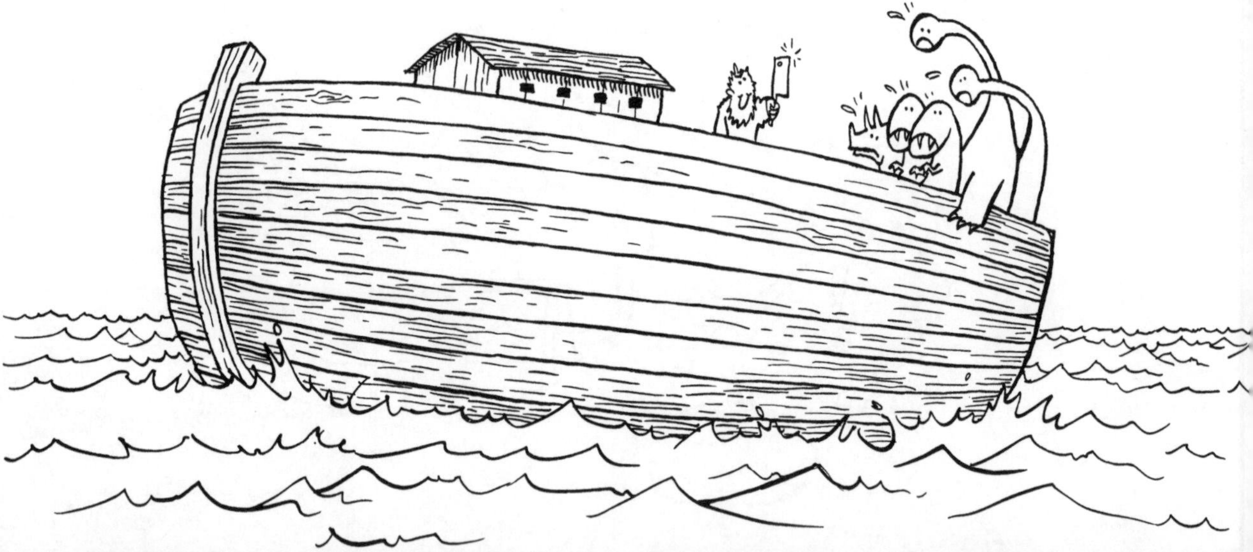

CAN YOU SPOT THE EIGHT DIFFERENCES BETWEEN THE PICTURES?

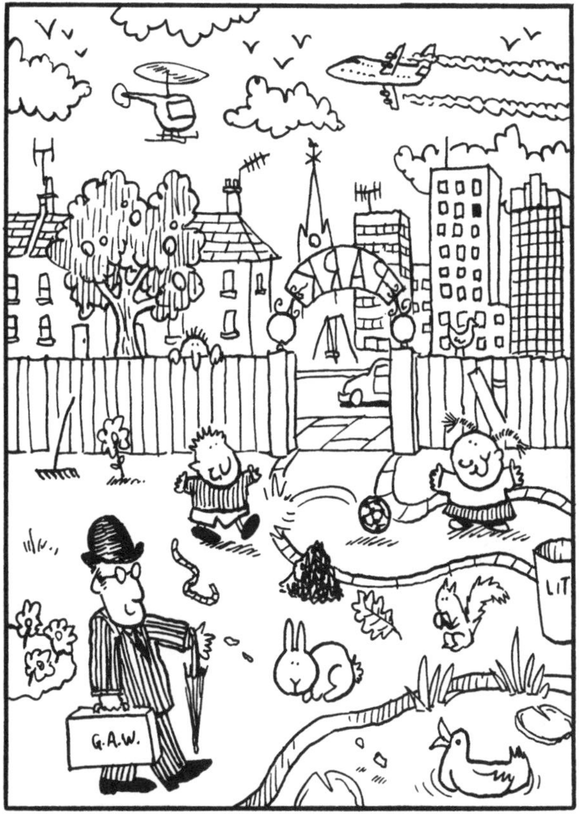
LIT
G.A.W.

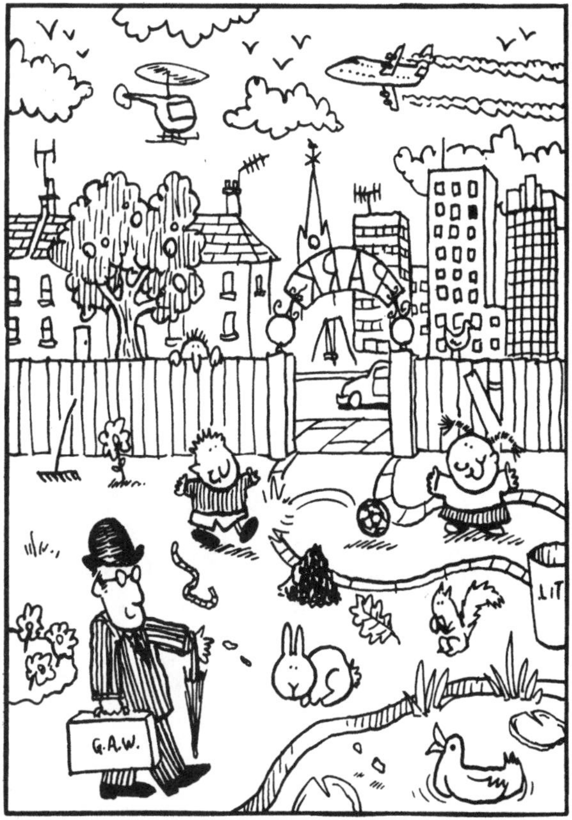
LIT
G.A.W.

SU DOKU IS HOW YOUR MUM RECEIVES CODED MESSAGES FROM HER COMMUNIST MASTERS

OVER 2500 CLOUDS CRASH EVERY YEAR

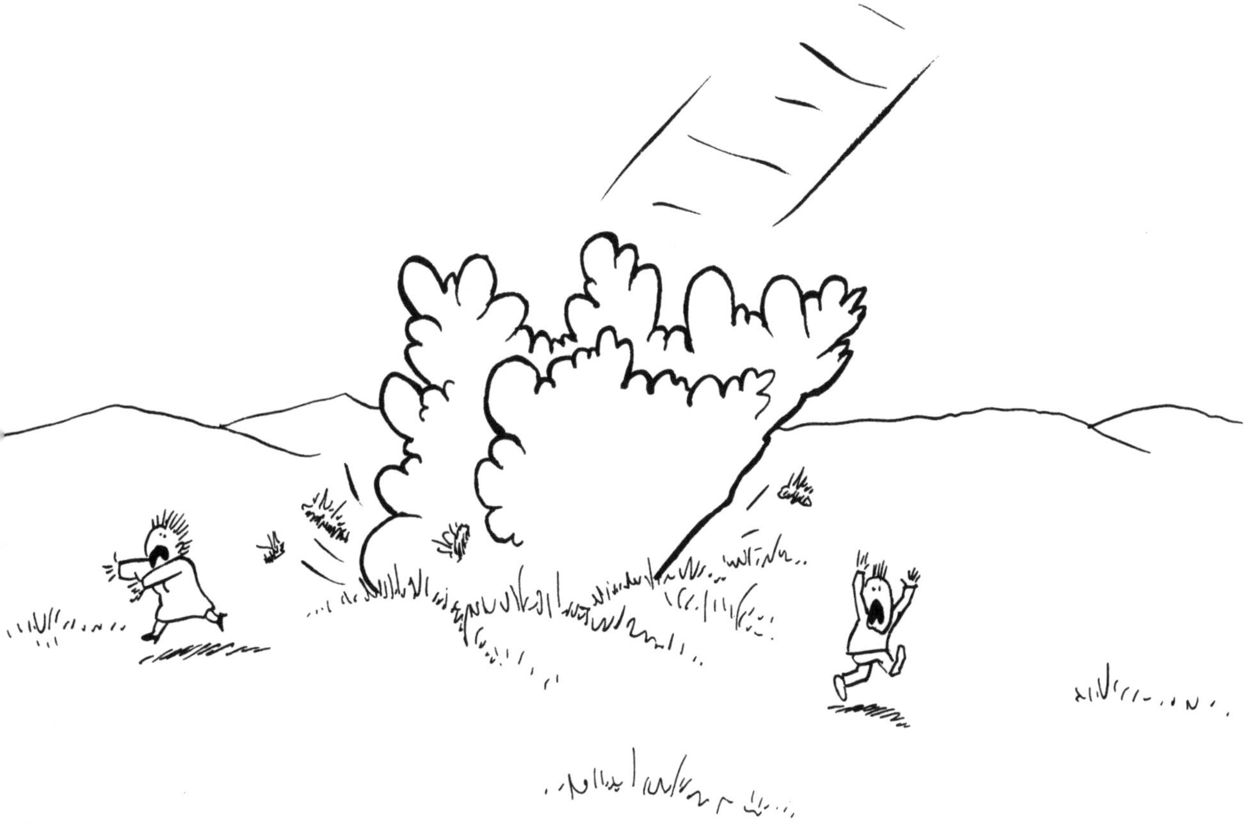

IF DR. DAVID BANNER
GETS SLIGHTLY ANNOYED
HE "HALF-HULKS"

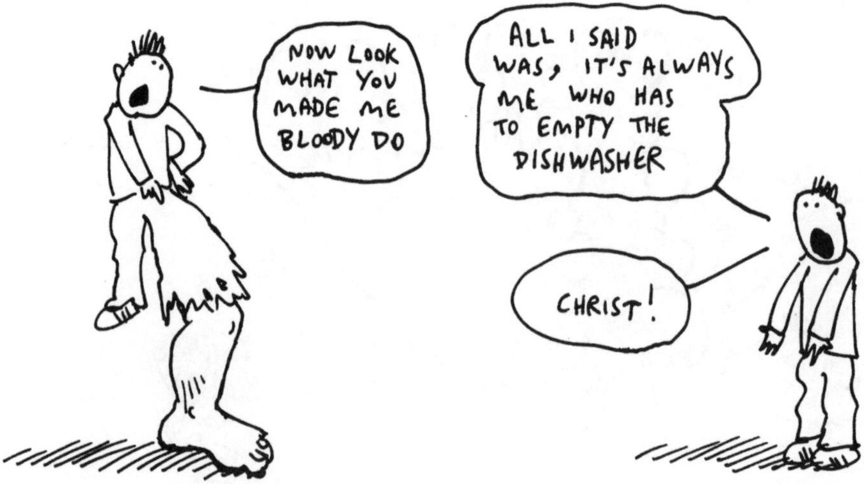
NOW LOOK WHAT YOU MADE ME BLOODY DO
ALL I SAID WAS, IT'S ALWAYS ME WHO HAS TO EMPTY THE DISHWASHER
CHRIST!

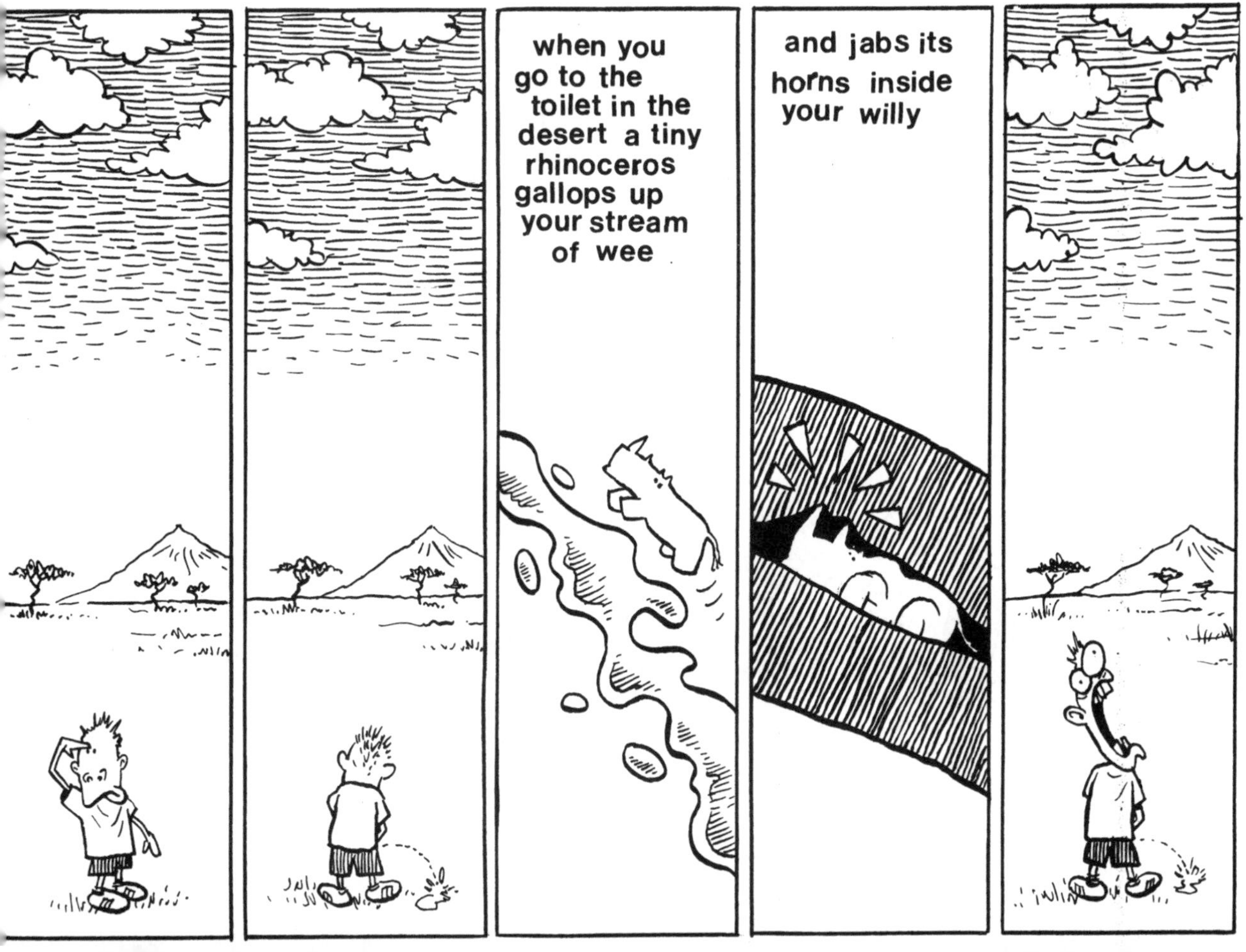
when you go to the toilet in the desert a tiny rhinoceros gallops up your stream of wee
and jabs its horns inside your willy

THE CRAZY GOLF COURSE AT WEYBOURNE, NORFOLK, WAS THE FIRST IN THE COUNTRY TO BENEFIT FROM A COURSE OF PSYCHOTHERAPY

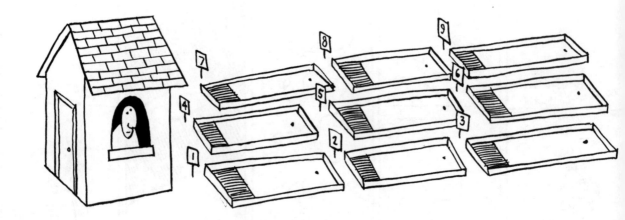

i just watched the six o'clock news

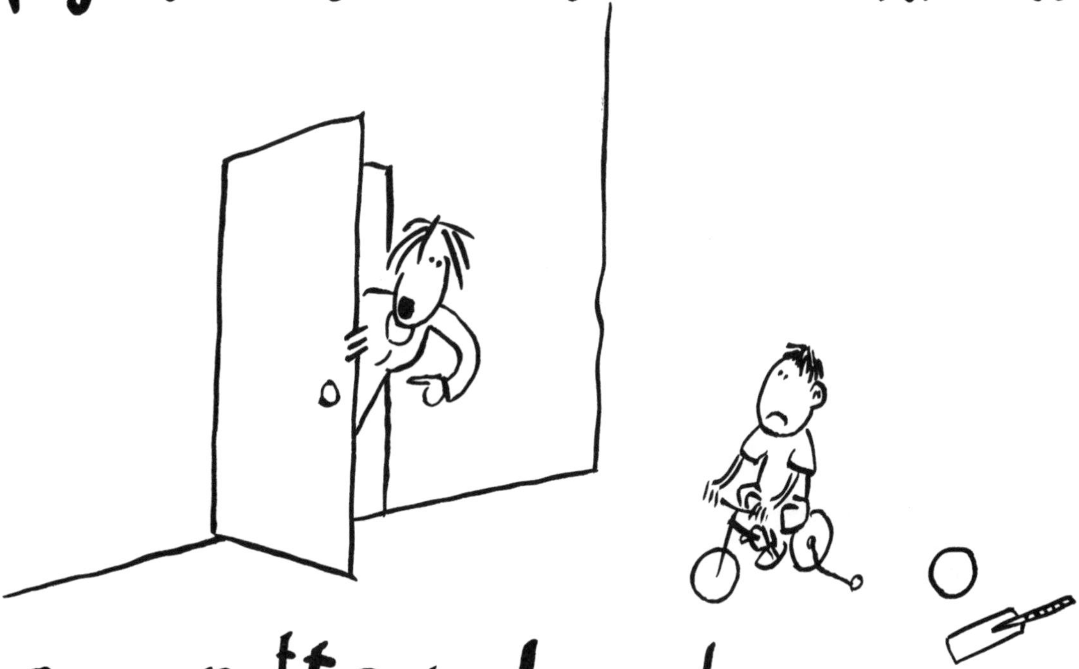

harry potter's been burned at the stake

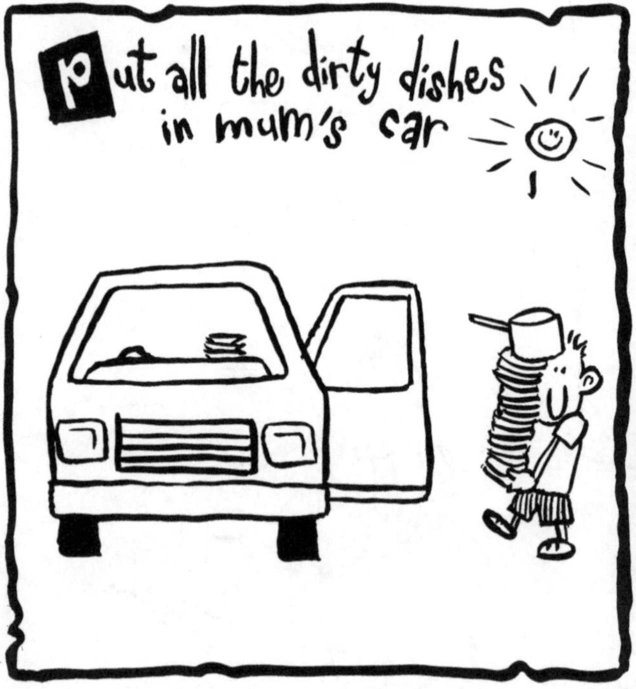
put all the dirty dishes
in mum's car

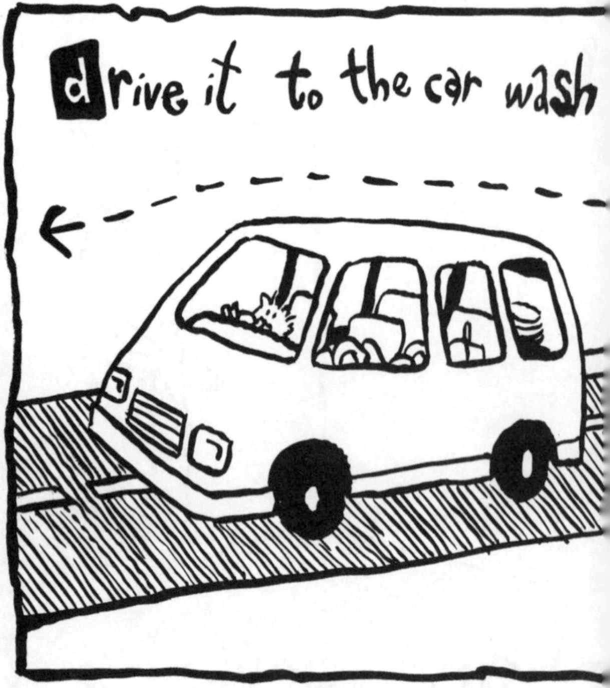
drive it to the car wash

Open all the windows and the sun roof before you go through

When you get home you'll have cleaned the DISHES, the CAR and YOURSELF!
mum will be so happy

IF THEY NAME A HURRICANE AFTER YOU YOU HAVE TO PAY FOR ALL THE DAMAGE IT CAUSES

BREAKING NEWS
HURRICANE LEON: LATEST

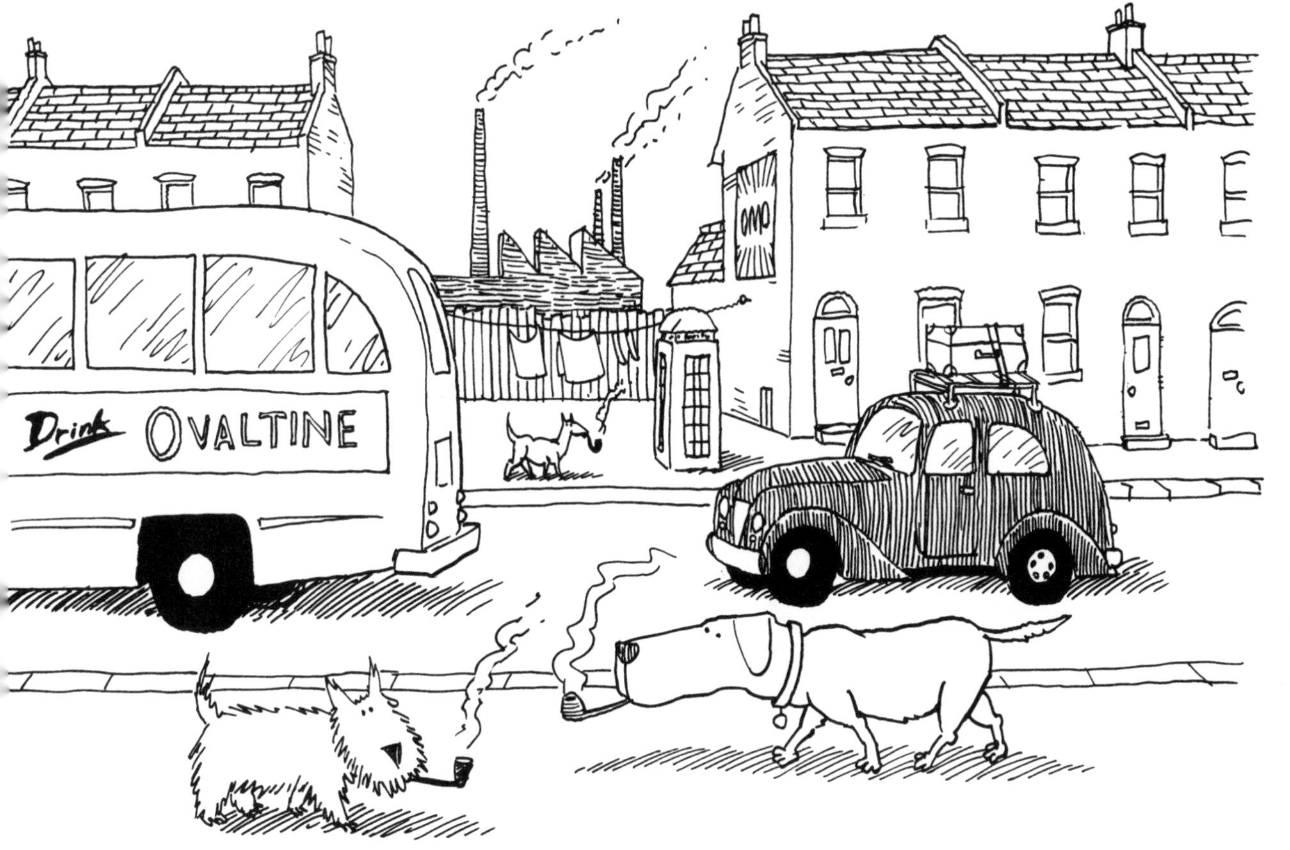
Drink OVALTINE
OMO

DOGS ALL SMOKED PIPES IN THE 1950s

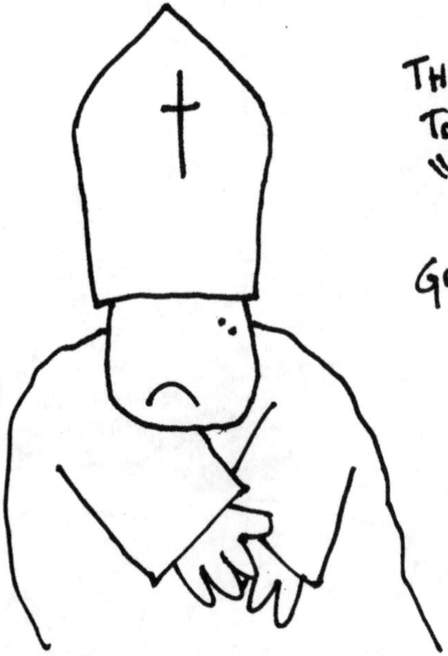

THE POPE ALWAYS HAS
TO RING GOD FOR THE
"WEEKLY CATCH UP"

GOD NEVER RINGS FIRST

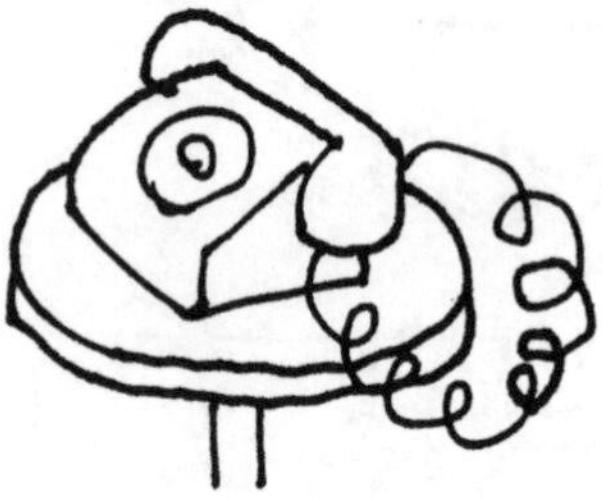

FOR THE WHOLE OF 1975, CHARLES M. SCHULZ SET HIS 'PEANUTS' STRIP IN THE AFTERMATH OF A NUCLEAR ATTACK

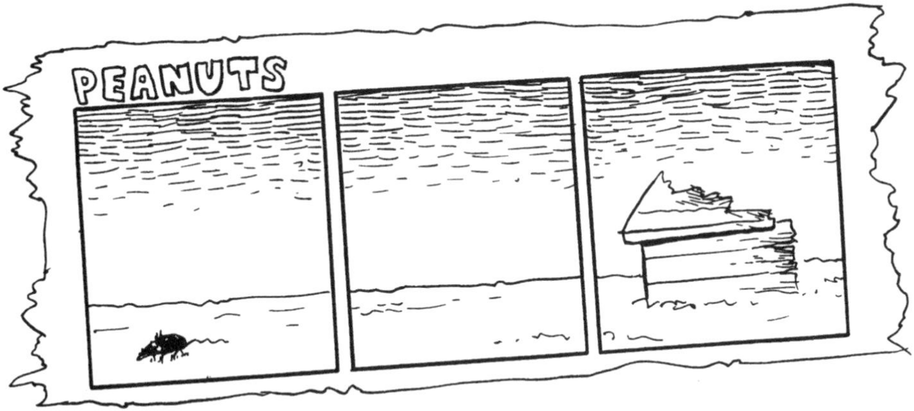
PEANUTS

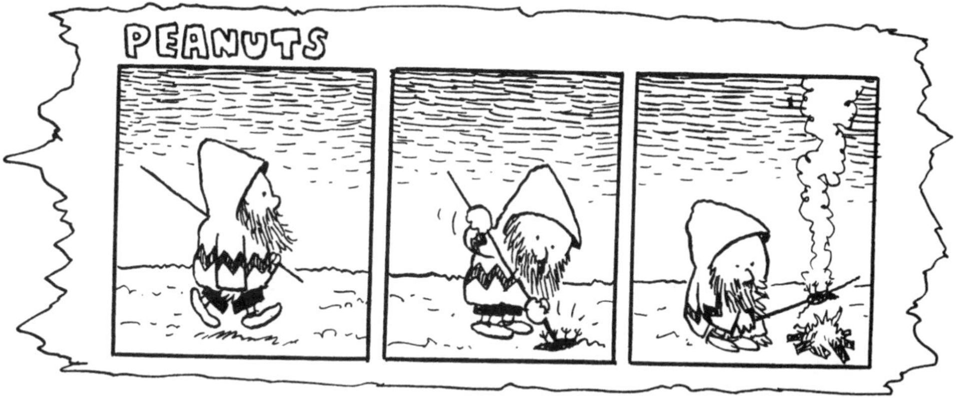
PEANUTS

where rubik's cubes come from

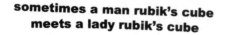

sometimes a man rubik's cube meets a lady rubik's cube

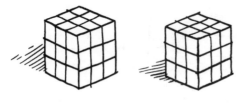

and if they like each other very much

they have a special hug

and soon they have a lovely family

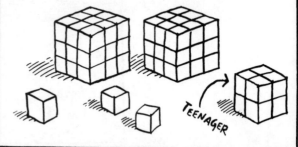

TEENAGER

WRITE DADDY'S NAME ON THE SIDE OF HIS CAR AND IT'LL BE EASIER FOR HIM TO FIND IT AT THE CAR PARK

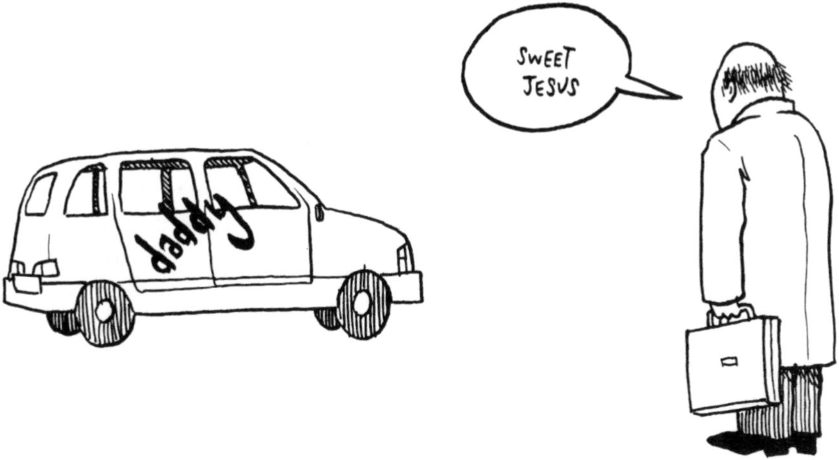
SWEET JESUS
daddy

HE'LL LOVE YOU FOR IT

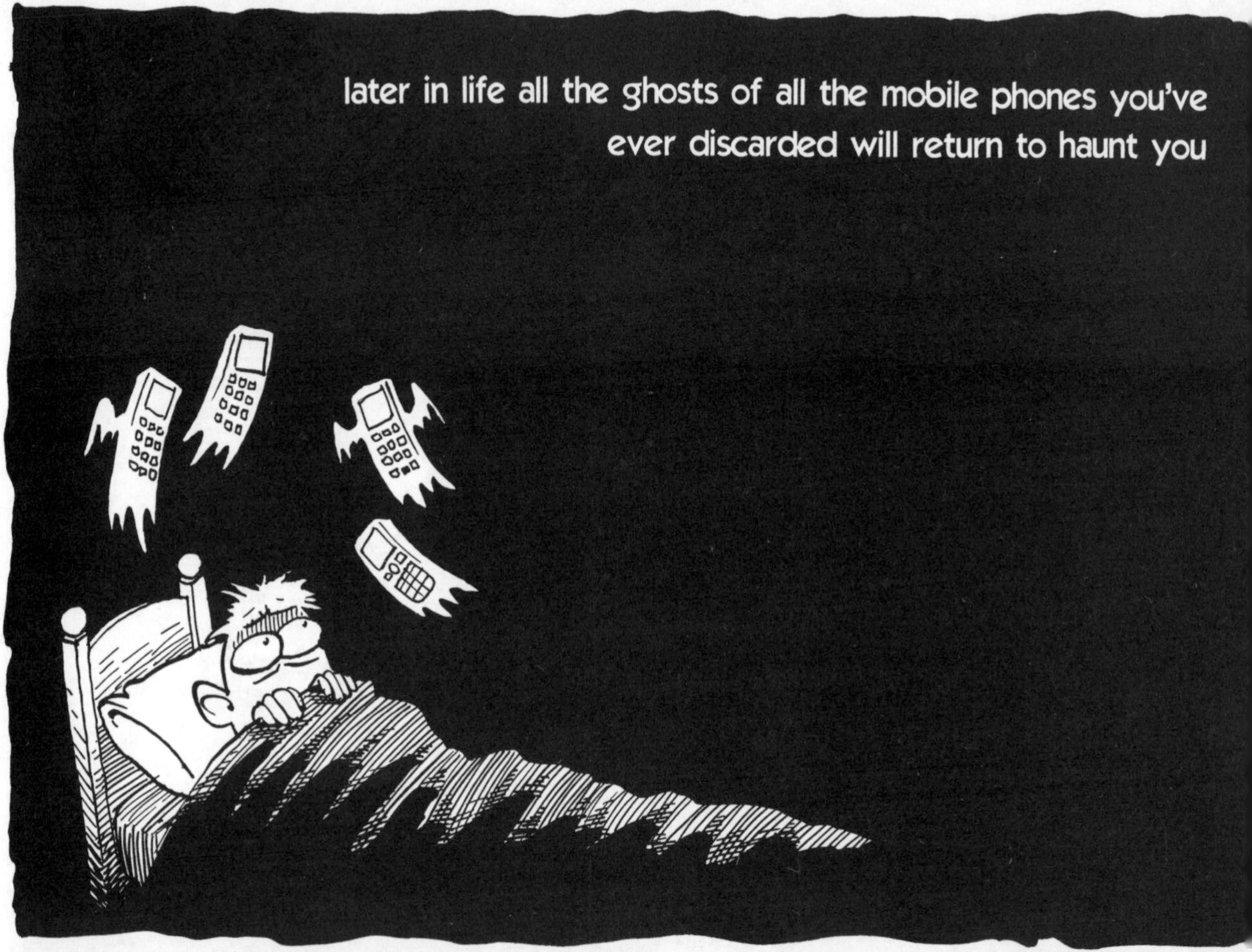
later in life all the ghosts of all the mobile phones you've ever discarded will return to haunt you

EVERYONE HAS TO TAKE A TURN AS THE PRESIDENT OF THE U.S.A.

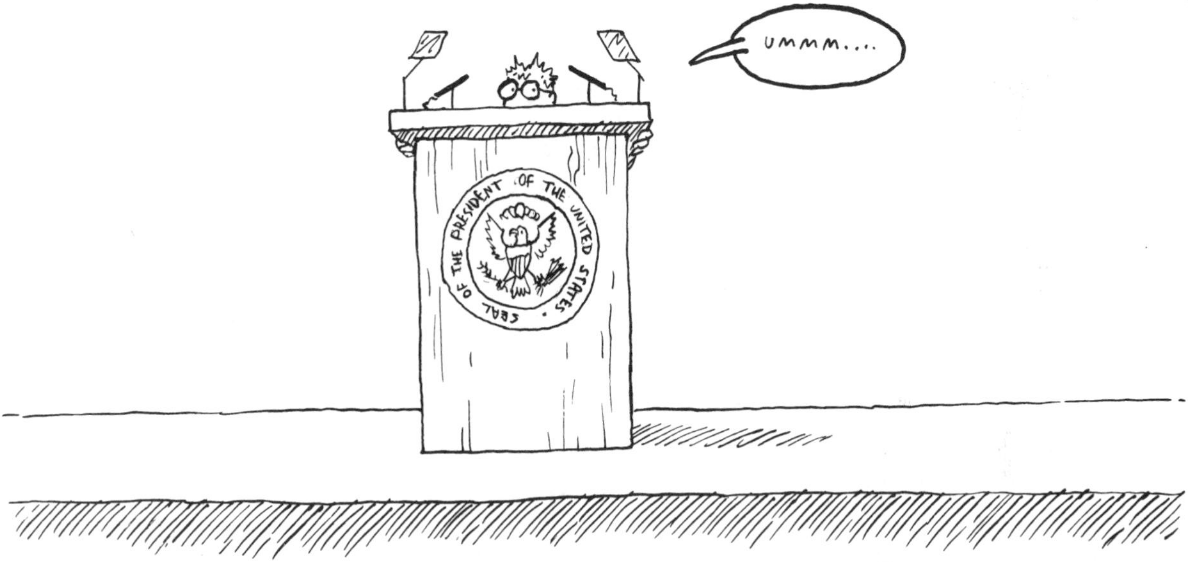
UMMM....
SEAL OF THE PRESIDENT OF THE UNITED STATES

YOU'RE ON IN 2011

YOU'D BETTER START RESEARCHING FISCAL POLICY OR YOU'LL BE IN BIG TROUBLE

ALL PANPIPE BUSKING GROUPS ARE CENTRALLY CONTROLLED FROM A SECRET BASE IN THE PERUVIAN ANDES

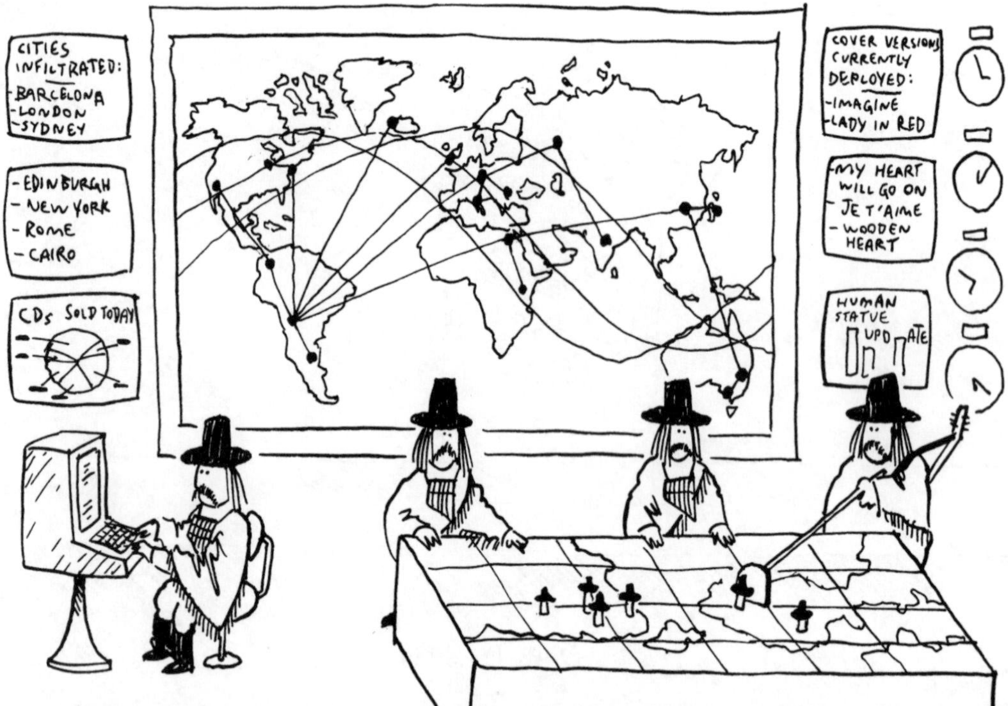
CITIES INFILTRATED:
-BARCELONA
-LONDON
-SYDNEY
- EDINBURGH
- NEW YORK
- ROME
- CAIRO
CDs SOLD TODAY
COVER VERSIONS CURRENTLY DEPLOYED:
-IMAGINE
-LADY IN RED
-MY HEART WILL GO ON
JE T'AIME
- WOODEN HEART
HUMAN STATUE
UPD ATE

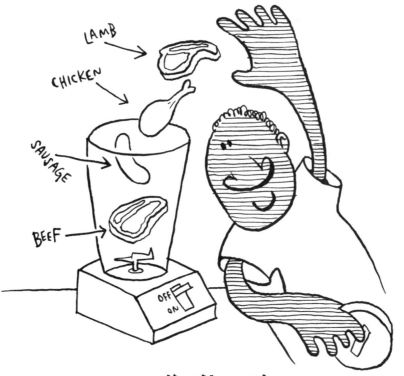

LAMB

CHICKEN

SAUSAGE

BEEF

OFF
ON

EVERYBODY LOVES A
MEAT SMOOTHIE

TRAVEL THE WORLD ON POCKET MONEY

ADDRESS A POSTCARD TO A DISTANT COUNTRY YOU'VE ALWAYS WANTED TO VISIT

NOW GLUE YOUR HAND TO THE POSTCARD AND GO TO THE POST OFFICE

NOW THEY'LL HAVE TO SEND *YOU* THERE TOO AND ALL FOR THE PRICE OF A STAMP

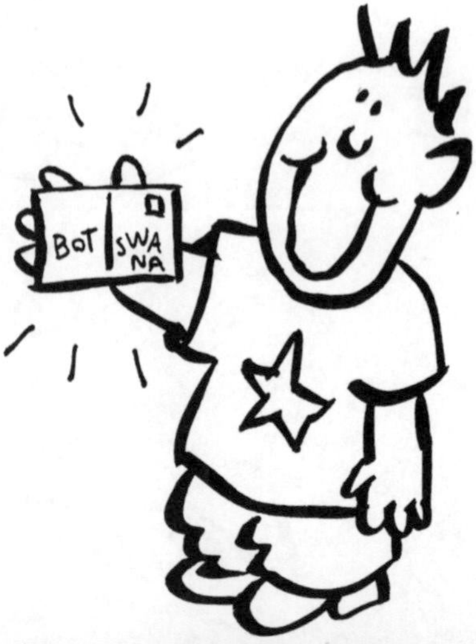
BOT SWA NA

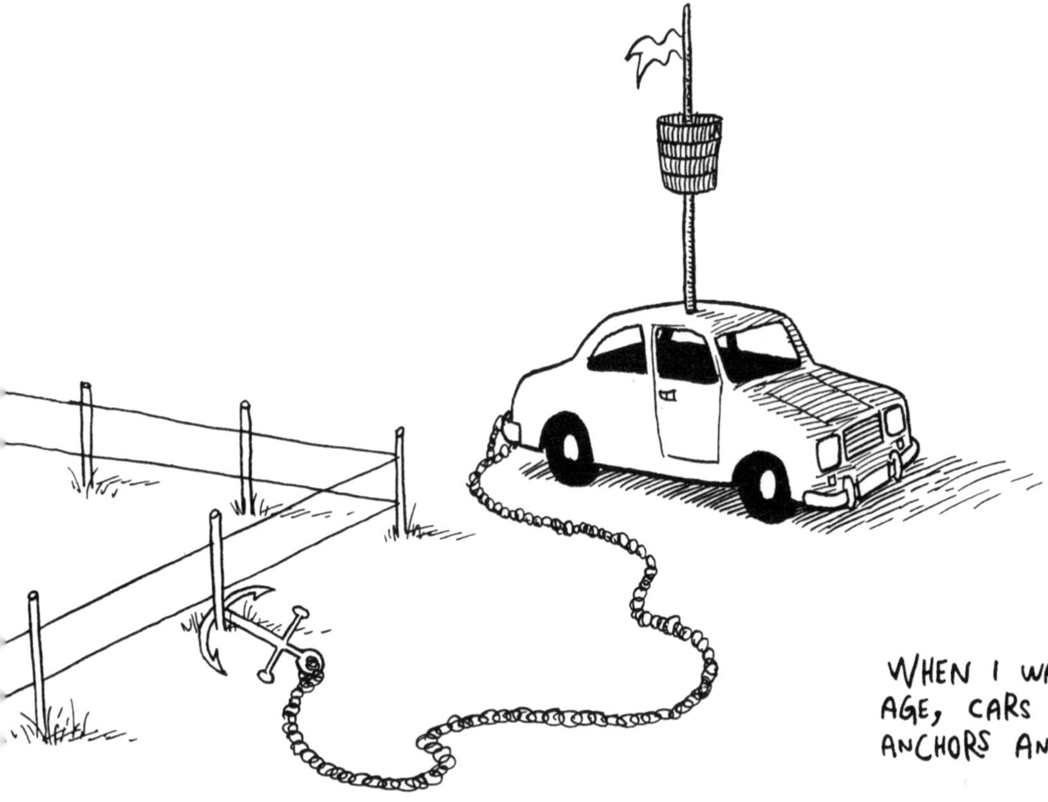

WHEN I WAS YOUR AGE, CARS ALL HAD ANCHORS AND TOPMASTS

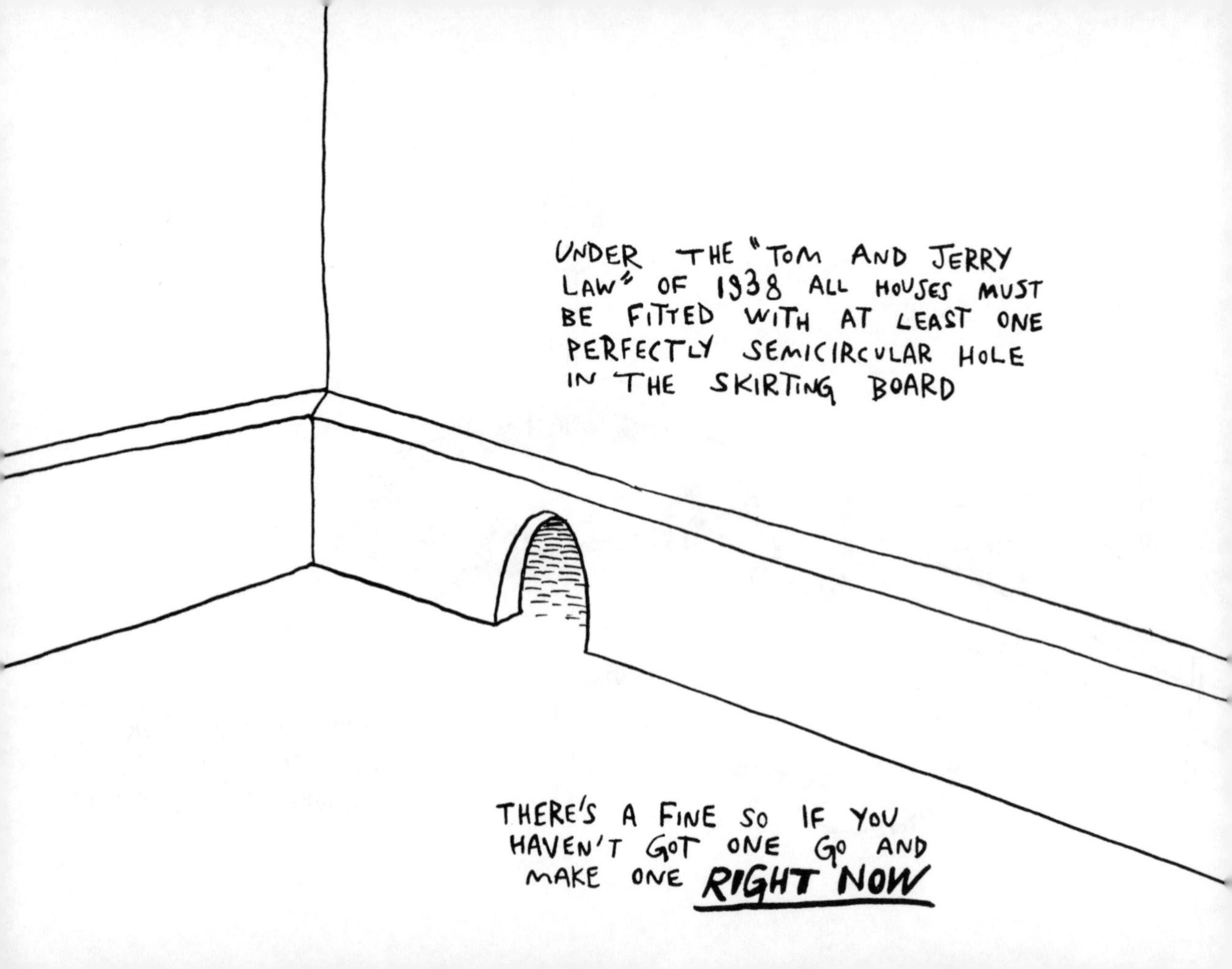
UNDER THE "TOM AND JERRY LAW" OF 1938 ALL HOUSES MUST BE FITTED WITH AT LEAST ONE PERFECTLY SEMICIRCULAR HOLE IN THE SKIRTING BOARD
THERE'S A FINE SO IF YOU HAVEN'T GOT ONE GO AND MAKE ONE RIGHT NOW

YOUR UNCLE MATTHEW HAD
HIS LEGS SURGICALLY FLARED
IN THE 1970s

JUST FIVE YEARS LATER HE
HAD THEM SURGICALLY
DRAINPIPED

FILL IN YOUR NAME ON THIS CARD:

Jupiter belongs to:
CUT HERE
CUT HERE

YOU ARE NOW THE KING OF JUPITER AND ALL ITS MOONS. CUT OUT THE CARD, LAMINATE IT AND CARRY IT WITH YOU AT ALL TIMES

RULE WISELY

THE TELETUBBIES HAVE THEIR OWN 'PETE BEST', SACKED JUST BEFORE THE OTHERS GOT FAMOUS

HIS NAME IS 'BOKO'

HE IS NOW AN ESTATE AGENT IN LEEDS

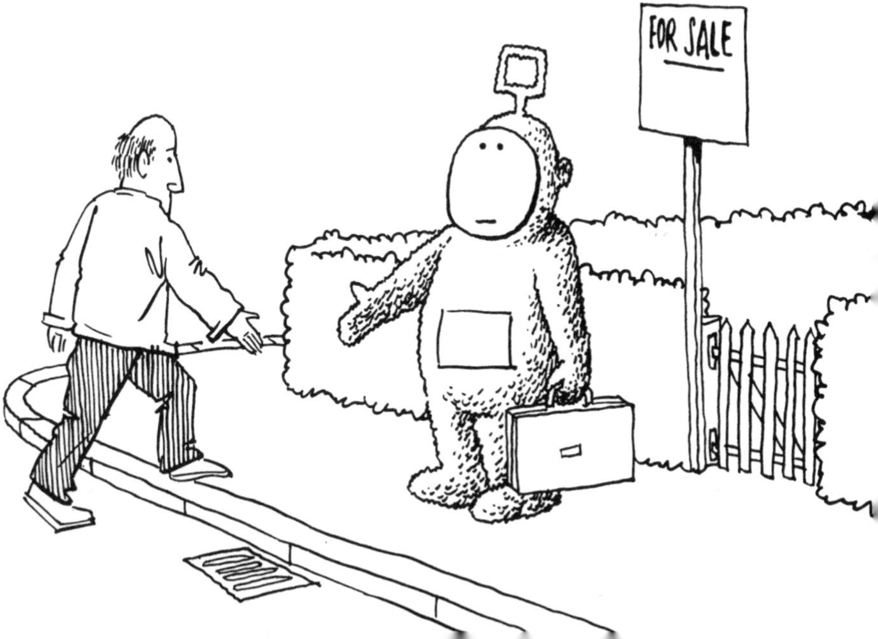
FOR SALE

Lego bricks are very communal creatures,
 living only to join up with other bricks

keep a Lego brick on its own in a shoe box
 and you can watch it go slowly mad

DANGLE A CORNETTO
ON A PIECE OF STRING

AND IT WILL ALWAYS
POINT NORTH

AFTER YOU GO TO BED YOUR DAD PLAYS KEYBOARDS FOR KISS

6 P.M.

9 P.M.

CAUTION: THIS IS ACTUALLY TRUE FOR ONE CHILD
IN THE WORLD SO BE SURE TO CHECK

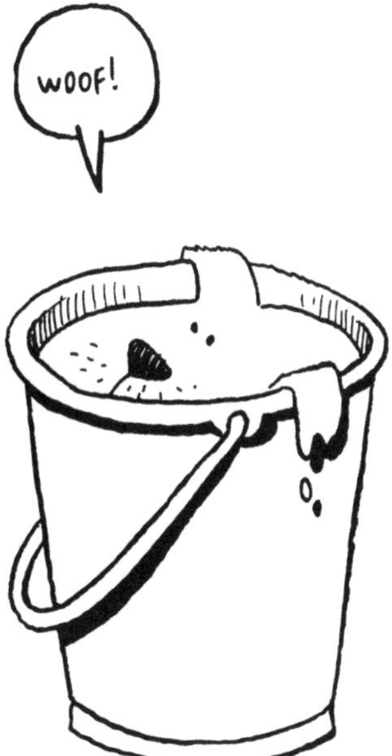
WOOF!

SCIENTISTS HAVE BRED AN ENTIRELY LIQUID DOG WHICH HAS TO BE CARRIED ROUND IN A BUCKET

ONE IN FIVE PEOPLE CAN FIT
THEIR WHOLE ARM UP
THEIR NOSE

ONE IN NINE CAN FIT IT
IN THEIR BELLY BUTTON

SHORT-SIGHTED PEOPLE WEAR
DOUBLE-GLAZED SPECTACLES
IN WINTER TO KEEP THEIR
FACES WARM ◎~~◎

father Christmas uses Amazon for the whole deliverin presents thing these days

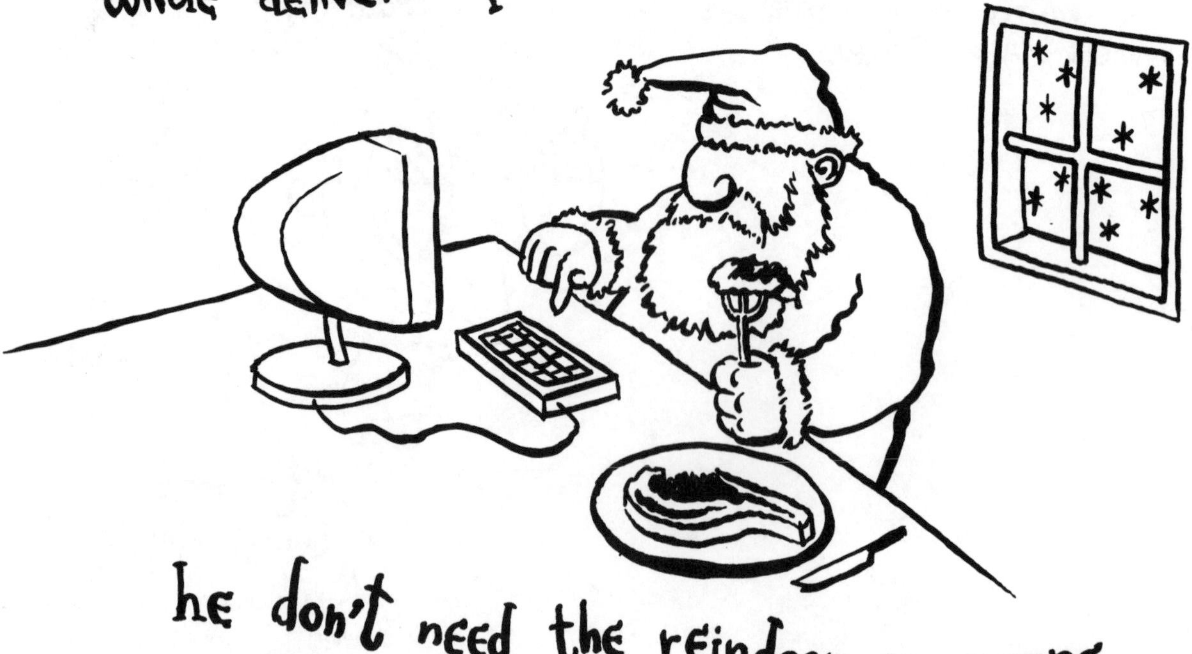

he don't need the reindeer no more

CHOCOLATE DIGESTIVES ARE **20,000** TIMES MORE LIKELY TO BE STRUCK BY LIGHTNING THAN NORMAL DIGESTIVES

BUT GO AHEAD, HAVE WHICHEVER YOU WANT

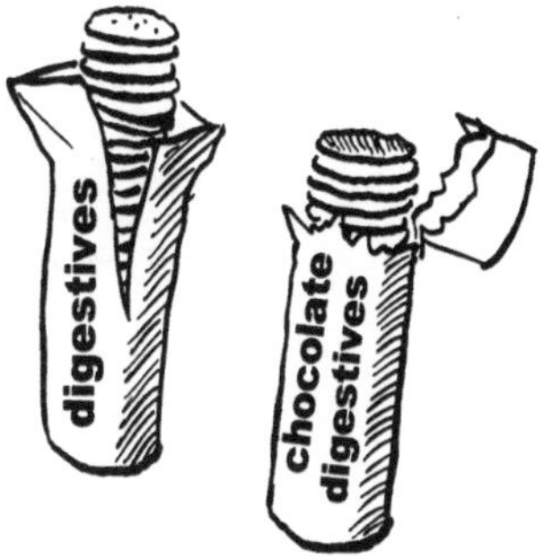
digestives
chocolate digestives

WHEN THERE'S NO MORE ROOM IN GINGERBREAD HELL
THE GINGERBREAD ZOMBIES WILL WALK THE EARTH

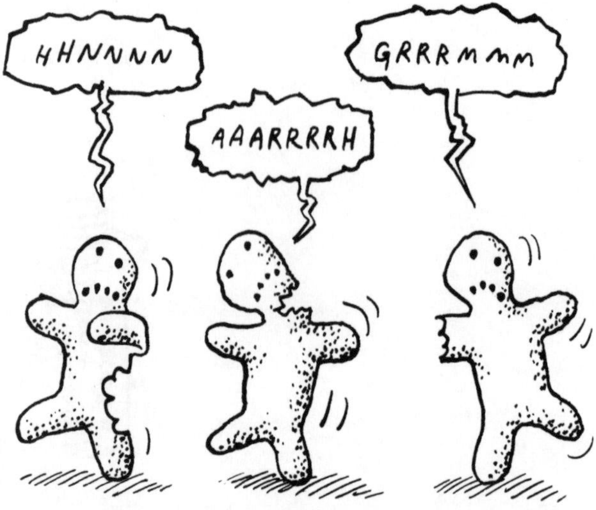
HHNNNN
AAARRRRH
GRRRMMM

(REMOVE THE HEAD OR EAT THE CURRANTS TO STOP THE CREATURE)

THE END

BONUS FACT: JESUS'S "CHRISTMOBILE" ONLY APPEARS IN TWO OF THE FOUR GOSPELS

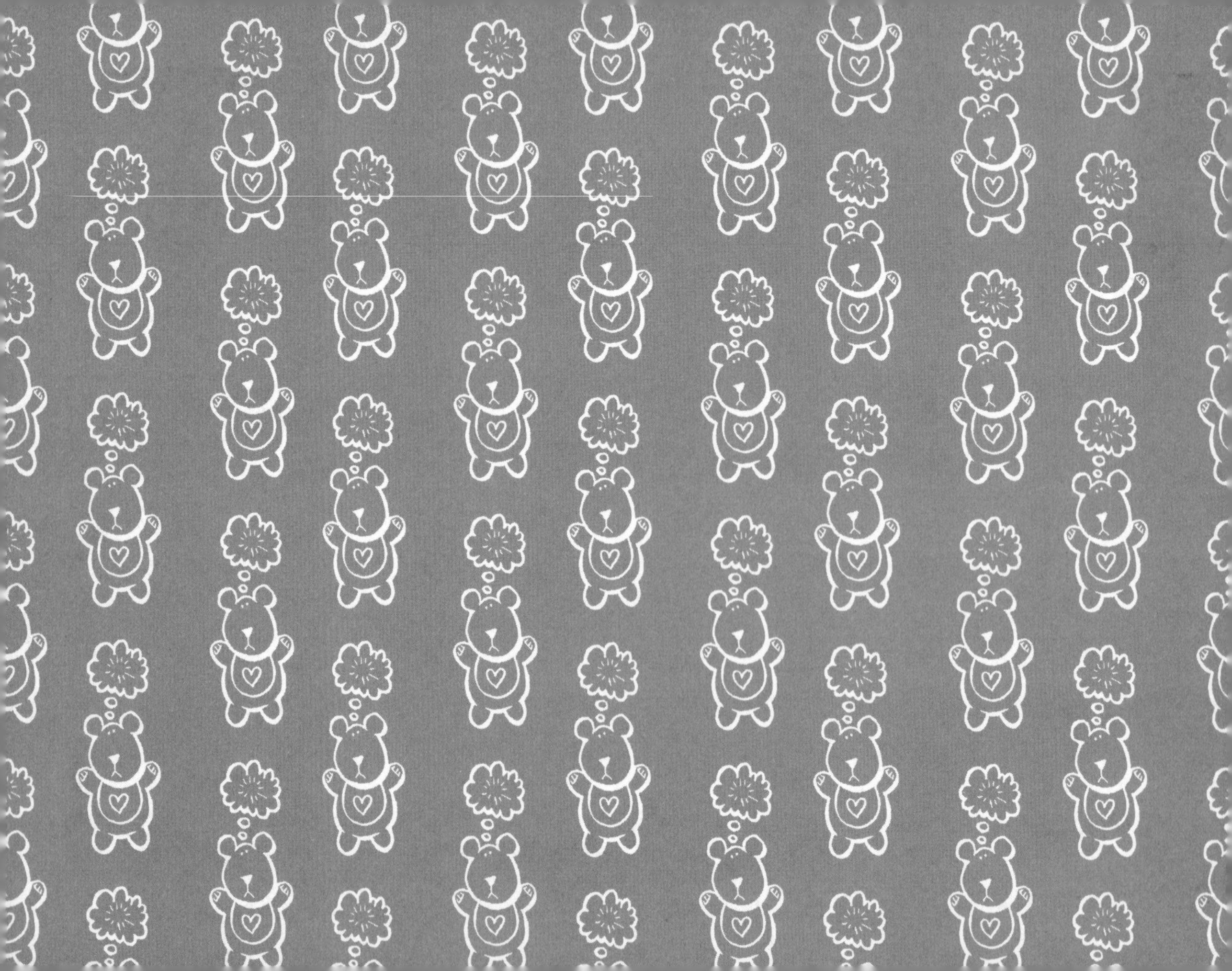